A Year in Ink

Volume 10

SAN DIEGO WRITERS, INK

A YEAR IN INK

ANTHOLOGY VOLUME 10

Edited by Judy Reeves

THE
INK SPOT
PRESS

A Year in Ink, Volume 10 is a publication of

The Ink Spot Press
San Diego Writers, Ink
NTC at Liberty Station
2730 Historic Decatur Road
Barracks 16, Suite 202
San Diego, CA 92106

Special thanks to Kristen Fogle, Kim Keeline, Matthew Phillips, the first
readers, and everyone else who helped shape this book in some way.

Cover art:
Ascendance by Patrick McMahon
PatrickMcMahonArt.weebly.com

Cover and layout design:
Arin Winkler
www.WinklerDesigns.com

ISBN: 978-0-9799204-9-3
Printed in the United States of America
Printed by Lightning Source, Inc.

Contents

Introduction

We go to our desk or table or we find a tuckaway in a corner or a make-do set-up in the garage or attic or basement or under the stairs or out back in the shed. We pile pillows behind us in bed or slouch on the couch; we load our laptops or iPads, or notebooks or journals, and we walk, we bike, we drive, we trolley to the café, the library, the bench in the park, the spot on the beach, the hideaway in the hills. Before dawn, before bed, after hours, after work, after all. We play music or we insist on silence. We go it alone or we do it together. We join a class or a workshop, a group or a gaggle. We conference, we symposium, we retreat. The kids are at school. The baby's sleeping. The cat. The dog. The chocolate. The coffee. Does anyone smoke anymore? On assignment, by inspiration, sudden flash or deliberate urge. First draft, third draft, who's counting draft. We write. We write and we write and we write. And out of that—our stories, our poems, our essays, novels and memoirs: This Anthology.

It is an honor and a delight, a challenge and a privilege to serve as editor for the tenth anniversary edition of *A Year in Ink,* the San Diego Writers, Ink annual collection of prose and poetry. For the debut anthology, in 2007, while serving as Executive Director of Writers, Ink, I worked alongside Editor Thomas Larson, as we set out to produce an anthology that would showcase the best work of writers in our community and serve as a beautiful and concrete representation of our organization's mission—to nurture writers and foster a literary community.

In 2008, we began the practice of inviting both a prose editor and a poetry editor to select from the hundreds of submissions. That year I was honored to work with Arthur Salm and Sandra Alcosser, who took on those roles and set the standard for what was to follow—eight more publications that have continued to represent the diverse, imaginative, many and lively voices of those associated with San Diego Writers, Ink, who use the written word to make their art and tell their stories.

Sixteen more editors would follow—eight prose (Jennifer Silva Redmond, Laurel Corona, T. Greenwood, Anthony Bonds, Jim Ruland, Bonnie ZoBell, and Dean Nelson) and eight poetry (Roger Aplon, Jerico Brown, Brandon Cesmat, Michael Klam, Shadab Zeest Hashmi, Sydney Brown, and reg e gains) and now we arrive at *A Year in Ink, Vol. 10.* I'm humbled to be among these talented and accomplished writers and poets who brought forth the beautiful anthologies that preceded this one.

Like those editors, I was glad for the guidance of the many first readers who volunteered their time and expertise to sift through the 238 blind submissions and offer their comments. Out of those and over many weeks and much deliberation, the work of forty-one writers was selected—eighteen poems and twenty-three works of prose—fiction presented in both flash and short story, excerpts from novels, and nonfiction in flash as well as longer memoirs and narrative essays.

I was pleased to discover, after we'd made our selections and authors' names were revealed, that poems by three of this year's writers—Regina Morin, Una Nichols Hynam and Seretta Martin— had also appeared in *A Year in Ink, Vol. 1,* as had a memoir excerpt by Patrick McMahon, whose stunning photograph serves as our cover art for this year's book. Reggie, Una, Seretta, and Patrick aren't the only writers whose work has appeared in more than one anthology. A quick glance through the tables of contents from all ten editions will confirm, that from its beginning, San Diego Writers, Ink has been a place for writers to join in community and that, for ten years, *A Year in Ink,* has been a voice for our community.

It's one thing to make the final selections of what pieces to include in any anthology, but then comes the challenge, both creative and practical, of determining the order of their appearance. It's always a joy to work with Executive Director Kristen Fogle, whose opinions and judgment I found so helpful as I struggled with choosing between this excellent poem or that one by the same author (honoring the policy of only one submission by any one writer), or whether to place this story before that one or after, as I attempted to shape the collection into a graceful arc that revealed its own story as each of the individual pieces told theirs.

The collection begins with Penny Wilkes's poem, "Becoming Marco Polo," which, for me, illustrates our approach in beginning any new work. Each one a dare, an exploration, an adventure, which is what I hope this collection will be for you as you read through it.

I hope, like me, you'll be charmed by the narrator in Ruth Roberts's story, "Killin' Chickens," and, like me, haunted by the lyricism of J. Dylan Yates's beautiful "you can taste and swallow but you may not digest."

Maybe your heart will go out to Joel, the protagonist in Greg Johnson's story, "Level 1," like mine did, or be cracked open by Leonora Simonovis-Brown's poem, "Still Life with a Baby." Maybe like me, you can't wait to find out what happens next in Dare DeLano's novel excerpt, *The Dance of the Paper Lanterns.* And if you like a touch of magic in your prose, as I do, then you'll find it in stories that, each in its own way, contains some: Jan Thompson's, "Hadewig Stylites," and Anthony Jesse's, "The Merry-Go-Round."

Within these pages are stories of home—being present in a single moment as in Carrie Danielson's wonderful poem, "Home Palindrome," or returning, as does the narrator in Krishna Jagannathan's "Sunday Breakfast," or leaving with the protagonist in Marty Eberhardt's novel excerpt, *Holding the Line: An American*

Family in Saigon. You'll find anger expressed in some of these works as well as lust and revenge, sex and desire, sins and forgiveness. Here are stories of war and its terrible effects, poems of loss and death, of love and beauty. Characters, real and imagined, invite you along for an adventure or to remember with them, another time. Our friendships, our families, our kindnesses and our cruelty. Our compassion, our hopes, and our dreams. All part of the human condition—all contained within these pages.

—Judy Reeves, January 2017

SAN DIEGO WRITERS, INK

A YEAR IN INK

ANTHOLOGY VOLUME 10

Becoming Marco Polo

Penny Wilkes

Outside her childhood bedroom,
a jacaranda tree rubbed the porch railing
in squeals that lead curiosity like a piper.
She sneaked out the window to climb it.

Thighs squeezed the bark; arms in hug.
She needed to touch the V formed by branches
near the ground. If only she could reach it,
then swing to the grass where adventures waited.

Night warbling continued from the tree. Muggens,
the cat, dug claws in the wood and scampered
the highway at will. Her tail spiraled in the breeze.
Finch chittering rose from limbs. Even they

flew in and out of branches or captured ants
on this Silk Road. A hummingbird made its nest
higher than her reach. When her father called,
she looked out the window, stuck in the middle.

Again she tried, clutched with her fingers
to find security in the roughness. Blood mingled
with gray bark in failed attempts to settle into the V.
Courage grew in welts on arms and legs.

In spring, an explosion of lavender blossoms

flew a fragrance of musk into the air. She took a breath
and tried once more. One shoe felt the wedge.
Another stretch and both feet arrived.

She balanced and looked upward into an applause
of leaves. She jumped from the V
to explore the world and back before dinner.

Dropping in the Eight

Tania Pryputniewicz

Back wheels propped against vertical wall,
board hanging free out over the bowl—one foot on,
one foot off—three times my ten-year-old son

hesitates, looks up to make sure I'm watching
through chain link fence. It kicks up a panic
in me akin to walking beneath blimps

or swimming in the open sea. When I nod,
glance away in respect, he commits, vanishes
below concrete lip to decisive click

of front wheels' contact and silver rhythmic
scroll of his arc. I listen for his proportion
of momentum: what he gathers on descent

must also propel him out onto far side's rim.
Practice doesn't help: the fear never goes,
he tells me, no matter how many times

you drop in. The thirty-somethings behind
skate park's desk agree, ringing up Gatorade
for sweaty dollars they push wrinkled

and upside down into plastic cash register
between coaching newbies and spraying

disinfectant into helmets. My son undoes

chin strap, dirt and sweat streaking cheek,
knee and elbow scabbed with yesterday's
dozen attempts to clear cone and grab

edge of board with one hand to stick
landing, his thumb a mottled salmon red
sanded and bleeding into his grip tape.

Killin' Chickens

Ruth Roberts

The rooster crow at first light. Before anyone see the sun in the sky. Full throat yell, head back, jubilant. Happy to be alive.

Rustlin' awake on my straw-fill mattress, I imagine his red comb rakin' the sky as he cock-a-doodle-doo. How he get ready for his call, I wonder? Do he have to shake himself awake, blink the sleep out of his eyes before he sound off? How do he come to? All in a start or stumblin' around? Coughin' to clear his throat first? Garglin' a little trough water to warm up? Maybe I sneak down some night before any light in the sky and spot him in his roostin' place in the tree and watch the whole show. I laugh at the idea of peepin' on him, knowin' I never get up that early to see the full performance.

He be just a bird. But what a bird. Outrageous! Of course, what do he have to worry about? He not goin' to be eat, unlike the hens roamin' around on the ground. As soon as their layin' slow down, they be on a short course to the stew pot. Plus Mr. James love that rooster. Call him "Red" and cluck to him to come when he walk by. Say, "He's too old and stringy for eatin'. Besides I've had him too long to let him go." He talk about him to anyone who listen.

Red be through with his tasks for the day. He shake everybody up good. Soon the mockingbird, the other butt-struttin' shouter, take up the job at his post on the highest limb in the neighborhood and run through his stolen song book over and over, keepin' everyone awake and on the job, challengin' everyone to try to go back to sleep. Except Mr. Rooster. He go back to bed, happy in a full day's work done.

I didn' want to think about all I had to do today, so I let my mind slip away to dream in the warm, cozy covers another little while. Then the big job of the day hit me. It wouldn' let itself be disremembered. Sure, that why birds fillin' my mind. I be goin' to learn how to kill a chicken today, chop its head off, pluck its feathers, gut it, butcher it and get it ready for the center platter on the Sunday dinner table. I watch Mama do this often, even help fetchin' water, buildin' a fire, pluckin' feathers, and spillin' guts, but I never struck the blow before.

Mama already out of bed. She jump out right when Red first crow. Mama always jump, eyes wide open, at the first sound of the rooster. I like to drift up slow, and Mama usually give me a long moment to dream before startin' in on me.

"Anarchy, come alive. I want to see your feet hit the floor," she say.

I hear Mama pull off her night shift and put on the dress she hung from the peg by the door the night before. I think about the dress I be havin' soon, not a hand-me-down child shift, but one made just for me from the blue chintz.

Mama pull in her breath to say my name again, irritation clear in the rasp of the intake. "I'm risin' up, Mama," I whisper and half sit up, slidin' one leg off the rustlin' cornhusk mattress, puttin' one foot on the cold floor. I jerk it back, but then rush both feet out, stand up and run, quick, quick, to my shoes lef' on the other side of the room. I hate those shoes, shapeless, rough buckskin with drawstrings around the ankle to hold them on. Soon I have a dress with shape, then I ask for shoes with heels, soles and buttons. Shoes with shape.

Mama say to me the other day, "Anarchy, you gettin' some shape on you. My girl goin' to be fine lookin' in her new dress." I giggle. It remind me of somethin' I hear over at the stable. Old Ben, the stablemaster, nod at the banker's young red-headed wife when she walk across the courthouse square, and say, "Look at that chassis on that lassie. She walk like a phaeton pulled by a fine, high-steppin' Tennessee Walker." The bright gleam on his face shine around in the other men's faces that turn to look.

I ponder the comment for awhile. The woman be the buggy or the horse? Both, I guess. That be fun, to walk by and have people compare me to beautiful things. I already know people stare, sly like, so I won' catch them. My bright skin color and hazel eyes pull them in, and then my right eye, veerin' in to peer slightly to the center of my face, when I look at them straight on with the other eye make them turn away from me quick. Mama call it my lazy eye, but she say it don' mean that I be lazy or even that my eye be lazy, it jus' have a mind of its own. People who be around me enough to see the eye ask me all kind of things about it like can I see the future, can I see what be behind me, and do I mind lookin' at the side of my nose so much?

Even Mr. Rob be curious. When he look at me straight in the face the first time, he say, "Amblyopia. That is the word for the condition of your eye. Two Greek words combined together. Meaning 'dull eye.' I've always wondered about such a case. Do you have the sense of seeing in two directions at once?"

"I don' think so."

"Well, perhaps we can do some experiments to find out. Very interesting."

I feel proud about my eye when he tell me this. I tell Mama about the wonderful new word he tell me for my eye so she can stop worryin', worryin' all the time about, "can I see good and straight," worryin' when I drop somethin' that I will break a dish and never be allowed to serve the table again. Always warnin' me "be careful, your eye," and "try extra hard."

Amblyopia. My word. A word just for me.

I think I will tell Jeremiah about my word. Maybe it will stop him from thinkin' I be spyin' on him because he can' tell where I be lookin'. I can tell those people who seem to think I be lyin' about somethin' or that my eye be evil. I can tell the preacher at the camp meetin' who say I ought to straighten up and stop goofin' off.

But Mama say, "Why he givin' you a word?"

"It for my eye, Mama, make it alright."

"No, don' make anythin' alright. Don' talk to him or anybody else about it."

Mama confuse me. I think she be happy that my eye rate, be special, instead of just sorry lookin'. I know she worry about my eye keepin' me from doin' work right and bein' good.

In truth, my eye didn' worry me that much. It didn' wander *all* the time. I couldn' exactly control it, but I did let it wander on its own sometime. It be likely to wander when I be thinkin' about somethin' off in my head and not puttin' my mind on specific matter. I feel I have the right to think when I want to, and if my eye go off and scare everbody else, including Mama, that just be too bad.

At times, my eye actually help me out. Miss Amanda be in a flustery mood and screw up her mouth and accuse me of not lookin' at her when she be talkin' to me, of not payin' attention, sayin', "I'm not going to put up with your impertinence and impudence," but then Miss Amanda slacken her mouth and drop her head and I know she remember that I can't help the wanderin' eye.

Mama say Miss Amanda has somethin' of a sof' spot for me that come and go. Mama tell me stories from when I be a baby that show how Miss Amanda feel. "Now Miss Amanda have no baby of her own for a few years cause Mr. James be old when she marry him. You be such a cute little thing with soft brown curls I fluff up with my hands, warm brown skin and those gray green eyes with one slippin' to look at your nose. You slep' in a cradle in the kitchen so I could nurse you and rock you and talk to you while I be cookin' and cleanin'. Miss Amanda sit at her pigeonhole desk jus' off the kitchen in the hallway keepin' the books for the jail and the farm. She see you lyin' in front of the stove and watchin' the flames through the isinglass door. You smile and gurgle, blow bubble, laugh and clap your han' when the door be open and the flames flare up. If I be busy when you be fussin', Miss Amanda get up and come and rock the cradle or pick you up and cuddle you and fluff your hair until you quiet down. I barely get you back from her. Then Miss Amanda has her own baby, and Mr. James' nephew Amos come to live with them. But she never have a little girl, and I see her ever now and then lookin' at you with her old sof' smile."

***

Now Mama be havin' me test out my wanderin' eye on chicken killin'.

After Mama and I fix Miss Amanda and everyone a quick breakfast of cold biscuits, country ham and red-eye gravy hot from the skillet, we walk the half-mile down the tree-lined dirt road to the chicken yard at the Mount farm.

"We killin' two chickens, got company comin' for Sunday dinner and all our family eat good, too. Then the scraps go to the jail."

"It like that song, Mama, 'Oh, we all have chicken and dumplin', when she come.'" I sing the song and dance a skippy step to offset my nerves.

Mama put her hand on my shoulder and say, "Calm down. Don' make so much noise. Where you get that song?"

"I hear them singin' it when they dig the trench and put up the fence at the farm. Jeremiah, Amos, and the others. Who the 'she' who come?"

"That jus like our old church song about Jesus comin' at the end."

"The end?"

"Yeah, you know. Rapture. Drivin' six white horses when she come. End of the world. Don' know who the 'she' is."

I walk the rest of the way deep in thought with chickens and Jesus all mix up in my mind.

***

Mama already has two chickens picked out in a chicken wire pen at the farm. "Layin' dropped off considerable from every day to about once a week. So these be eatin' chickens now."

I watch as Mama catch one, hold it upside down by its legs, wings flutterin', squawkin' complaints. She walk over to a stump of wood about waist high with a hatchet sunk into the choppin' block. Pullin' the hatchet out with her right hand, she whip sling the chicken over her head and slam its head down on the block. I want to cover my face cause I know what be comin', but I don'. With her right hand, she bring that hatchet down on the neck of the stun chicken with one eye bulgin' out to the sky and in one stroke, chop the head off. The chicken legs start kickin'. She fling that chicken and it run around the yard, flappin' its wings, lookin' for its head. Finally, the chicken drop and be still. Mama's face be hard, annoyance mixed with deep disgust. She pick the headless chicken up and throw it in the bucket.

With her firm face, Mama say, "Now your turn, Anarchy."

"What if I can' hit its neck?"

"You chop it again. Don' miss the first time. It just get worse."

Mama reach for the second chicken, now squat down in the farthes' corner of the cage. She grab it by its legs as it flap and squawk and hand it over to me and say, "Here, take it legs and swing it over your head and whap it down on the block."

With horror on my mind and holdin' my face as far away as possible, I do as I be told. Those legs cold and scaley in my hand. The grasp, twirl, and slap down just come out of me like Mama do, my mind somewhere else. When I look down, I see it work. The neck slam down on the choppin' block. The chicken one eye stare into the sky in silence.

"Now here's the hatchet." The blade be splash with chicken blood, but the handle be clean.

"What if I hit my hand?"

"Don'."

"What if my eyes don' line up and I don' see it straight?"

"Get to it. Make your eyes work right."

I take a couple of practice swipes to get the range and swing back and bring the hatchet down as hard as I dare.

The cut be sure and clean and the head fall off, the eye stuck open.

I do it. Hallelujah. The legs start kickin'. I fling the chicken, claspin' my mouth with my empty left hand, my right hand grippin' the handle of the hatchet, blood drippin' toward the ground. I watch the chicken flap and run 'til it collapse and die.

"Mama!" I cry.

Mama grab me in her arms and say, "You do good. Your eyes line up just right. I tell Miss Amanda you can do all the jobs you need to. Then when hard times come a knockin' at the door, we all stay together."

On the way home, Mama carry the bucket of two chickens ready to pluck, butcher, and cut up into fryin' pieces. With the sharp metallic smell of blood in the air, I think of the other verse to the song I hear my brother and Amos sing, "Oh, we'll kill the old red rooster when she come."

But nobody be killin' Red, I argue with the song.

I shudder to think about how bad things be if we got to kill that old bird.

The Y

Michael W. Berns

Every Tuesday we swim naked at the Y—it's the Nyack Boys School rule.

When JB, the headmaster, has sick call, I try to get out of swimming.

"I have the sniffles, sir." He always turns me down.

Today Wolfie and me head down Broadway to the Y early so he can shoot baskets and I can practice underwater swimming. He's clumsy, and I don't know how he manages to get the basketball into the hoop. Maybe that's why he's on the basketball team and I'm the scorekeeper. But I can swim underwater on one breath further than anyone else, and that's why I'm captain of the swim team.

We kick pinecones along the sidewalk, trying to see who can kick them the furthest without them skidding into the street. We're focused on this when I hear shouts from behind. I look over my shoulder and see three townies barreling toward us. One of them calls out, "Hey, you NBS rich kids, we're gonna kick your asses."

"Shit, Wolfie."

"Shit, Berns."

We run like rabbits chased by a pack of wild dogs, make a quick right across Main, and weave through traffic. I see the truck's yellow, red, and blue balloons just in time to pull Wolfie back as the Wonder Bread truck screeches to a stop a few feet past us in front of the A&P.

"Geez, Wolfie," I shout. "We were almost toast."

The townies are still after us, and I say, "Quick, into Woolworth's and out the back door."

"How do you know we can get out the back?" Wolfie yells back.

"I stole ball-points last year," I say, as he follows me through the front door. We zip down the aisle past the cash register lady who says, "Hey," and we're out the back door, behind the Y.

We double over with hands on our knees, gasp a few times, and climb the iron steps of the Y's rear entrance, avoiding the front desk where we're supposed to sign in.

I strip in front of my locker and think about what happened last week. Coach Horvath had tried to teach us how to dive off the board. Most of the kids either ran to the end, stopped, and then jumped, or chickened out. When it was my turn, Coach gave a quick blast of his whistle so everyone would pay attention. "Okay, Berns," he shouted, "you're team captain, now show us how to dive."

I never dived from a board. I ran as fast as I could and took a big jump so I would land on the end of the board. It bent, and shot me up over the water. I stretched my arms in front, waited for my body to bend forward, but it didn't; I landed flat on my stomach. When I hit the surface, it was like someone smacked my belly and balls with a baseball bat. I dog-paddled to the side, hung there to catch my breath, and waited for the pain to go away. It didn't. My nuts hurt all week.

I shake the memory from my head and trot toward the smell of chlorine seeping under the door from the Olympic-size, indoor pool. My pecker is shriveled like a prune. My balls hang loose and bounce off my thigh. I want to get one underwater swim in before Coach and the other boys arrive.

I take a deep breath; push through the door, run to pool's edge and dive headlong into the water. I don't surface. I hold my breath and execute the breaststroke while kicking my legs like a frog. I follow the line on the pool bottom that marks the swimming lane—gonna try for two lengths without surfacing.

At the end of the first lap I'm pretty relaxed; do a perfect underwater turn and push off the wall for a second lap. By the markings on the bottom, I can tell I'm halfway there. My lungs burn so I concentrate on the black tiles. I release some air and speed up my stroke. I'm over the drain in the deep end—the wall's only a few strokes away. My lungs are ready to split and I have an urge to breathe in water, but instead I blow out the air from my lungs and take one final stroke. I bang into the wall and shoot to the surface.

My head pops out of the water like a cork, and I gulp in air. Then I hear cheers and screams. The chlorine from the water burns my eyes and everything's a blur but I can make out shapes of people seated in the enclosed observation section. Bodies about my size run alongside the pool, and others are seated on two long benches. I'm still gasping when I swim to the side nearest the benches. I drape one leg over the pool edge and pull my naked body out of the water. I flop onto my back and continue to suck in fresh air.

It's dead quiet.

I flip onto my stomach and look at the nearest bench. I rub my eyes to clear my vision; my heart jumps several beats. It's full of girls in red bathing suits with circular school crests in the middle, below tiny tits. I look down at my water-shriveled pecker, jump up, and dash around the pool toward the locker room accompanied by cheers, whistles, and hoots from the gallery.

I yank open my locker and throw up on my shoes.

Out of the corner of my eye I see Wolfie standing by his locker, and before he opens his mouth, I say, "Swallowed too much water."

"No swimming today," he says with a huge grin, and continues, "St Mary's and St Anne's reserved the pool for a swim meet, and all of NBS is watching. We missed the sign at the front desk 'cause we came in the back door. "

Level I

Greg Johnson

"Watch out," Joel said, "fat guy coming through." He slid aside a plastic post that held a short length of purple ribbon and stepped into the row of the football stadium reserved for the Homecoming court.

Sara Sveldon's and Leana Nolan's spidery legs jutted out from under their gowns as the Homecoming princesses back-crawled up into the laps of the students behind them.

"Maybe just a little farther," Joel said, "I'm not sure I can make it through."

They giggled. Joel wanted to believe they were giggling at what he had just said, and maybe they were. He had so little experience speaking to popular kids or any kids really.

He sidestepped down the row, his belly and thighs bumping the students in front of him. "Sorry," Joel said, sucking in his gut the best he could. Arriving back at his assigned spot, Joel sat down and his body spread over the bench like a giant water balloon.

Ross Wade, Prince Ross Wade, the surfer-looking boy from Joel's English class, reached over and punched Joel in the arm. "Where'd you go?"

"Bathroom," Joel said. But Ross had already turned away to speak to the girls behind him, and Joel, although grateful for the inquiry, was alone again.

Joel's crown, with its cherry-like marbles topping each spire, rested on the bench where he'd left it. He checked for dog poop or black shoe polish before putting it on. It sat high on his beach-ball head with only his curly red hair to steady it. Queen Jennifer Portmyer's crown, and Jennifer along with it, had been missing since early in the first quarter. Embarrassed to be seen with him probably, or bored to death because he'd only said two words to her, "Good one," when Springdale scored their first touchdown.

But Joel wasn't going to let that ruin his night. He'd had plenty of practice being alone. He could enjoy things without someone else confirming that they were enjoyable, and he enjoyed being at a football game. The light poles soared into a misty sky. Banks of bulbs lit the field like the alien landing site of his favorite video game, *Spacemen Eat Your Face*. And who knows, maybe flying saucers were approaching because the stands seemed electrified. Voltage charged the Springdale students until it arced from their mouths in screams and cheers and laughter. Joel kept quiet but he tingled as well.

"Hey, King Joel," he heard from somewhere behind him in the stands. "Your ass-crack is showing. Either that or someone moved the Grand Canyon." Laughter seemed to ripple out from the spot of the insult, as if kids needed the person next to them to laugh before they could laugh. Joel raised his hand, a thank you for acknowledging him and knowing his name. This was his new tack, ever since his nomination as Homecoming King: to go along, to act unhurt, to laugh along with them. When someone said, "You sure are fat," he would say, "Yes, and stupid too." Funny how easy it was to make fun of the fat kid, even when you were the fat kid.

Joel hoped his parents hadn't heard the ass-crack comment, and maybe they hadn't since they sat way up in the stands. They'd already worried enough. An hour before leaving for the stadium his mom began toothbrushing the kitchen grout in her good dress and his dad had sweat-circles under his arms.

Joel knew his ass-crack wasn't showing. Under his slacks and his pressed short-sleeved shirt, he wore a special bodysuit that extended from his lower thighs to his neck. It was stretchy and tight as a girdle because it was a kind of girdle. It kept the sway of his belly and chest in check, or at least it was supposed to.

As the clock ticked down to halftime his fellow Springdale Spartans went nuts with each snap of the ball. Joel went nuts too, on the inside. He loved the Spartans. He was a Spartan. The thump of the bass drum pulsed though the metal bench. The beat accelerated to the point where Joel wanted to leap from his seat, pump his fists into the Springdale air, and yell, "Go!" And when the brass section blared forth, every wonderful emotion squirted from his oversized glands: love, pride, power, peace. He loved football.

As a freshman he had played football for one week before Coach Ronkowski pulled him aside. "Joel, you have an anger problem. You don't have any." It was true. He couldn't make himself hurt anyone. His father had said, "Son, you're a peaceful person. That's a wonderful quality." But all through school the boys had called him a big fat sissy.

The announcer said, "Another long gain by number 23, Cam Wright." Cam was the running back, Jennifer's boyfriend, first runner-up for Homecoming King, and not a very nice person. During Joel's five days on the team, Cam had called him a lot worse things than big fat sissy. He and his buddies used to follow Joel to his locker, watch him change out of his jersey and his pads and talk about having sex with his folds.

So it was better that Cam was on the field and not sitting next to him, even though Ross had made room for Cam and left Joel isolated on the bench. Conspicuous, but Joel had always been conspicuous. He knew what the kids were thinking as they looked down from the stands. They had the same reaction now as they did in junior high as they did in elementary school: some kids felt sorry for him, some kids laughed at him and, baffling to Joel, some kids hated him. But that just was the way it was, and Joel, with his new way of thinking since being nominated, was okay with it. "No pain, no gain," Coach Ronkowski used to yell. Now Joel repeated it to himself. No pain, no gain. The players on the field took their hits and he would take his. He would be tough because he'd been handed a chance, his last chance in high school to have something happen.

Of course his nomination was a joke. He knew that. There was a good chance he was the least popular kid at Springdale High. Before the nomination you could have asked a hundred kids, "What's the name of that huge fat kid?" And probably all of them would have said, "I don't know. I've always called him The Fat Kid." But in the past few weeks a hundred kids had said, "Joel." "Hey, Joel." "How's it hanging, Joel?" And when other kids used other names, Your Royal Thighness, Sire Spare Tire, King K-cup, he would answer, "Yes, it is I, your liege. Goodwill to you, my minion." And it worked, partly because they didn't know what he was talking about, but mostly because he'd said something, anything. Silence was a painful place to live and Joel had moved out. He was in the game now, Level I. He'd been fortunate to acquire the crown, and, like the laser vaporizer in *Spacemen Eat Your Face*, it didn't matter how you got it, you just used it.

It was nearly halftime. Joel saw Jennifer in front of the bleachers, using the metal walkway as a runway. She had to be coming to take her place beside him, strutting, stopping, turning, waving, smiling, as the adulations tumbled down on her from the stands. Joel wanted to admire his queen like everyone else, but he couldn't stop worrying about the width of the four steps that led to the bottom of the bleachers and the shoulders of the students who sat next to those steps. Even at practice, with no shoulders in the way, it had been hard for Joel to negotiate the stairs with Jennifer on his arm. He would pivot with each step, flinging her back and forth. Carla Hernandez, the little sophomore girl who volunteered as Homecoming coordinator, told Jennifer, "Don't wrap your arm around his. Just hold on with your hand and quit complaining." Joel had smiled when she'd said that. She was almost like his friend. They'd spoken four times and two of those times had nothing to do with Homecoming.

Jennifer gracefully ascended the stairs and slipped past Sara and Leana, whispering something and making them laugh. She was beautiful. A little sturdier than her twig-like princesses but still slim. Her royal blue dress wrapped around her like a snake, hugging her hips, overlapping in front and parting to show her shins. And it veed down from her throat to her breasts, which, unlike Sara Sveldon and Leana Nolan, she had plenty of.

Jennifer sat down a foot away from the bulge of his hip. "Hi, Joel. It's almost time. Remember to smile." He peeked at his queen. She had chubby lips, and big green eyes outlined in black mascara. Joel thought about kissing her, not in a real way but in a fantasy way, his fat lips, her fat lips.

A loud boom shook the stands. Joel twitched. A cannon near the end zone smoked like a giant cigarette. The band thundered to life, marching in place near the cannon for a minute before high-stepping onto the field; and the cheerleaders, right down in front of Joel and his queen, kicked their bare legs higher than their heads, pom-poms jerking to the rhythm of the Springdale Spartans Marching Band. This was it, halftime. Joel, who had tried to hide his way through three years of high school, was about to take the stage.

The music stopped. The cheerleaders stood still. Their raised pom-poms pointed up to Joel and Jennifer, just as Carla Hernandez had instructed. "Ladies and gentlemen, boys and girls, it's Homecoming here in Springdale." The announcer paused as the people in the stands stood and stomped and cheered. "Please welcome to the field the Homecoming king and queen and their court."

Joel took a deep breath and stood. Sara and Leana stepped out onto the stairs and climbed up two steps to let the king and queen lead the way. But Jennifer was getting away as Joel's hip bumped into the faces of the kids who had turned to watch.

"The king and queen, ladies and gentlemen, Joel Peters and Jennifer Portmyer."

Screaming, whistling, howling—the whole student body went crazy. He and Jennifer were like rock stars, well maybe Jennifer more than him, but that was okay. He caught up to her at the stairs. She put her hand into the sweaty crevasse near his elbow then quickly slid it out and pinched his shirt.

Joel rocked to the step below, and Jennifer hopped down beside him.

As the cheers faded he heard the underlying laughter. Of course it was there. He got so caught up in the excitement he forgot he was The Fat Kid.

"They're collapsing," someone yelled. "The stairs are collapsing."

"Hail to King K-cup. Hail to thee."

Joel raised his free hand, "Yes, thank you," but he didn't dare look up and lose sight of the next step.

He made it past the shoulders to the walkway at the bottom of the bleachers. Now only four more steps down to the field, and they were wider. The tug of Jennifer's fingers pulled at his shirt. Three, two, one, his foot sank into the grass.

When Joel finally allowed himself to look up he saw Cam. His uniform bore the mud marks of battle. He stood like a gladiator, feet apart, helmet neatly tucked under his arm.

"You're an embarrassment, you fat pig," he said.

Sometimes it was hard to stick with the rules, to remember how Level I worked, because all Joel's instincts told him to look down and keep walking. But he stopped and faced Cam. "Can you be more specific, Hampshire, Duroc, Javelina?"

Jennifer pulled Joel forward by his shirt sleeve, and Cam took the arm of Sara Sveldon. They lined up like a wedding party, king and queen in the middle, Cam and Ross beside Joel, Sara, and Leana beside Jennifer. A few thousand people watched them from the bleachers.

Carla trotted across the grass and handed Jennifer the microphone, and she stepped forward in her royal blue wrap-around dress and the crown nestled perfectly into the swirl of her blond hair. "Hi, everybody!"

Joel didn't listen to Jennifer's speech. He'd heard it several times at practice and he had his own to worry about. But before he got halfway done telling himself everything would be okay, Jennifer thrust a fist into the air.

"Thanks, everybody." Her face was not only beautiful, but more joyful than any face Joel had ever seen. "And remember," she said, "Spartans rock, Spartans win, and Spartans rule!"

The crowd hooted, clapped, and some guy yelled, "I love you, Jennifer!"

She smiled with her chubby lips. "I love you too," she yelled. And then she held out the mic for Joel.

Uh-oh. His turn. Just like in *Spacemen Eat Your Face*, he needed to concentrate and avoid the paralyzer ray. And he needed to remember Carla's advice: be expressive, look at the crowd, and don't hurry.

Joel took the mic from Jennifer's hand.

"Piggy," Cam whispered.

Joel ignored him for a second before he remembered his oath: respond to every word. He leaned toward Cam and whispered, "I loved her on *The Muppets*."

Before Cam could say more, Joel took a step forward and raised the mic. "Welcome all you Spartans, ex-Spartans, and parents of Spartans. And all you want-to-be Spartans across the field." Joel had made up the last part while his dad drove him and his mom to the game. The wild cheers and applause from the stands destroyed the few boos from the small set of bleachers behind him. "I guess there really are no ex-Spartans because once you're a Spartan you're a Spartan for life." That part was supposed to sound made-up but wasn't. Some people clapped. "Our senior class—"

"Fat!" Someone in the stands shouted the word so loudly and so clearly.

"Yes," Joel said. He lowered the mic and raised it again. "Yes, I..." He didn't know what to say. He lowered his head and looked at his shiny 13EEEE oxfords. It wasn't much of an insult, just the word that a thousand people thought and a few people said every day. But for some reason *Fat* had rendered him speechless. And when he decided not to respond, to forget the rules of the game and continue with the halftime show, he couldn't remember the words to his speech. At the fifty-yard line, in front of the entire student body and half the town, Joel just stood.

"Go Spartans," Jennifer whispered.

Joel looked at her.

"Go Spartans, say it," she said.

"Go Spartans," Joel said in a trance-like monotone, and then he held the mic out as if someone were there to take it.

Applause started high in the stands and slowly spread. It lasted a long time, long enough for Joel to recover and realize they it was meant for him. Embarrassing feel-sorry-for-the-fat-kid applause that should have made him feel worse but somehow made him feel better.

A hunched-over Carla Hernandez finally ran up and took the mic from his hand. The clapping stopped. Joel couldn't hear anyone laughing except Cam, and he could barely hear him. The procession exited the center of the field as planned. Jennifer waved with one hand and held his shirt with the other, but at the sideline she released him and trotted over to Cam. A whole gang of kids clanged down the metal steps to join Sara, Leana, and Ross. And the people in the stands stood and stretched or headed for the restrooms or the food shack.

The kids on the field closed ranks and Joel was left looking at their backs. His crown felt dangerously close to sliding off his head. He centered it and stood still.

On the edge of the field, in his white short-sleeved shirt, his thin tie, his big hoopy pants, he felt like a security guard. The king of security guards. A lonely security guard until his mom and dad appeared on each side of him.

"Hi, son. Good job out there," his dad said.

"Yeah, sweetheart. You did fine," his mom said. "And you added a little adlib to your speech. That was great."

His mom and dad looked as if they might have been the Homecoming king and queen of their day. His dad was slim and handsome, and his mom was every bit as pretty as Jennifer in an older-type way.

"I went blank," Joel said. His parents might be able to ignore what had happened, but Joel couldn't. He needed to work on his focus, play the game right no matter how many people are watching or how many Cams are saying bad things or how many people yell, "Fat." After all, all beginners fail during Level I and get their faces eaten. You just need to hit reset and start over.

They stood for a minute facing the empty field without speaking. Finally his dad said, "You know Joel, kids can be mean. You've done your speech, and if you'd like to call it a night and come on home, it would be fine."

"Yeah, sweetheart," his mom said. "It would be fine."

"No. I've got the rest of the game and the dance. It's a good game, huh Dad? Well, it's a blowout, but our guys are doing great."

"Yeah. They look really good."

The three of them stood quietly out of bounds at the twenty-yard line. It was going to be different his senior year. He would respond to every word spoken to him and he would make fun of himself. And before the end of football season, before Christmas, he would move on to Level II. And when someone said, "You sure are fat," he would say, "That's a mean thing to say." And someone like Carla Hernandez might overhear and think that he was honest and brave, and then they might talk to him. And by January or February he might sit at a lunch table with one or two friends, and they would talk and laugh just like other kids. And even if that didn't happen, even if he never progressed past Level I, at least the kids at school knew his name.

In the Fast Lane

Jill G. Hall

From the MGBGT's bucket seat I watch Greg strut out of the Tijuana liquor store and climb behind the wheel. Stick shift between us, he unscrews the tequila bottle's cap and offers me a swig. I shake my blonde head no. I'm impressed, no lemon or salt in sight, he raises the bottle and gulps golden liquid down, worm and all. He lights a joint and soon the car fills with smoke and steamy heat. No need for me to take a hit, at sixteen, I'm susceptible to contact highs. He lays the roach in the ashtray and we make out for a while. Led Zeppelin on the eight-track, he revs the motor, winds the car over muddy roads beside cardboard houses that melt in the rain, back to the border. There he rolls down the window and replies, "U.S.A." The bored agent peers in, ignores Greg's hand on my tanned thigh, the smell of weed and waves us through. He pushes hard on the gas pedal. A slick highway greets us. An orange sun floats like a buoy on the Pacific. The sports car speeds up, passes a VW van, a Pinto, a semi. In Chula Vista he yells above the music, "Let's get off." My heart races as he crosses over three lanes toward the exit and bashes the rear of a sedan. My eyes close tight and I hunker down as the car spins around and around and I'm sure we're going to die. I hear the squeal of tires, shrieking metal and my scream. Suddenly the car stops and so does the noise. Greg calls my name but I can't reply. My voice has disappeared. Car doors slam. A far-off siren wails. Someone touches my neck, lifts me out, sets me on my feet. It's dark now. A flashlight blinds me and my shivering body is wrapped in a scratchy blanket. Blinking squad cars reveal smashed vehicles on the freeway's side. I sit beside Greg in the tow truck and rock back and forth repeating The Lord's Prayer as the car, now an aluminum ball of foil, is hoisted up behind us. The driver climbs in and says to me, "Good thing you had your seatbelt on or you'd be dead." I nod my head not wanting to admit that I hadn't been wearing it. Greg didn't think they were cool.

you can taste and swallow but you may not digest

J. Dylan Yates

(For Matthew)

"a shell is a coffin for the wind" - Unknown

Small white shells,
Shell lined the edges of the large grey rocks—rocks that grew
along the cliff across the street from the house I got born into.
my abacus those little coffins,
my amulets,
my angels' playground,
my stone church on that beach below— waves crashing and
preaching.
placed with thoughtful fingers those,
six-, seven-, eight-, nine-, ten-year-old fingers, with thoughts that
were latent.
Latent thoughts for latent years.
Hunting a shell— the day's witness, then, palming delicate edges,
climb until I found a hiding place amid the rocks on the jetty, adding my treasure.
Hidden while my mother's flesh bruised and cut beneath my
father's fingers,
waves sounding over sirens.
Never hearing shrill screams on that beach.

> *Never smelling whiskey on those rocks decorated with ur-*
> *chin doilies.*

Smelling briny sea and foreign through those shells.

Wishing I could sing along to those sea songs,
before I learned I was, before I had a voice.

At eleven, in the late fall, long after the liberation of my father's
leaving,
> *gathering those coffins from their rock biers—all the small*
> *white shells with breathing holes.*
Pulling them out of order, off those rocks-their burial place.
They were unrocked,
> *reburied for safety in shoeboxes,*
and stuck in one of the mausoleum caverns created by the sea-
wall.

After winter, I went to pay my respects, but found they'd been
reclaimed,
> *those shells carted and tossed with shoeboxes,*
although all the years in their dormancy on the rocks, they—
closer to the edge of their birth, had remained unclaimed.

At thirteen I replaced the shells with a ring,
> *a promise ring,*
> *a ring that promised love from a boy,*
and placed that promise reverently on a rock, in a place I noted
but never found again.

Fourteen, watching friends in envy for their passions, wondering
> *where did my passion live?*
> *Only living in distance— feeding on distance.*
Longing for strong feelings, believing myself incapable, perhaps
broken.

Believing in the possibility, and then suspending disbelief,
>   *an audience role— I waited in the dark.*
>   *Watching them dance love-lit and inspired.*
>   *My applause— contentless sound.*

Fifteen and dreaming of
>   *seeing her again for the first time in this life;*
green eyes, a soft voice, only staying with me when I slept.
Believing and creating a world to separate this love from my reality,
>   *I awakened to realize that this body is a coffin for my soul.*

Seventeen,
>   *I am kissed*
>   *a blood-draining, everlasting-life-promising kiss in Green-*
>   *wich Village,*
>   *that wakes me from my latent.*
Finding my ring and tattooed on my body; promise kept— I've had my life since.

That woman was my teacher.
When class concluded I received a B+— highest mark in my class.
>   *I earned that grade in that class.*
But, when she handed mine, eyes averted, voice low— she cautioned, "Don't Tell Anyone."

>   *Don't tell.*
Don't tell?
I felt wild in that Village. I had found my voice.
That whole Village raised me, and brought me home, and taught me how to use handcuffs.
I had a few teachers that summer.
>   *Don't tell?*

Then my mother on the way to the dentist.

My mother, who after liberation hitchhiked to meet people in her
see-through blouses,
who lost her face in the rug during an acid trip,
who lived on an inheritance, but took food stamps to rip off the
ugly government and build her pharmacy— trading stamps for
valium and black beauties.
My mother who I thought, of all the nutty liberals, I could tell,
froze and changed the subject.

Thinking then, at seventeen,
I cannot place this on a rock it will be crushed and brushed away,
>   But then realizing even in a cavern within a seawall— hid-
>   den is not safe; I was found and rooted out in my shoebox.

So each lover counted my abacus, became my amulet, and growing stronger with each witness until I learned to sing that my body
is just a coffin for my soul,
>   I did tell.
>   I am undead; rising out of my coffin for love.
My blood is my own.
You can spill it. I will bleed the blood of thousands, maybe mil-
lions.
It will look like yours and you can taste and swallow, but you may
not digest.

When I am mirrored I can see myself in us.
We are undead— rising, all of us, out of our coffins,
>   like the wind through that shell.

She's Leaving Home

Colleen Brennan

My mother announces the good news to me over watery coffee and soggy macaroons. My seventeen-year-old sister Joanie is getting married! I interpret my mother's enthusiasm as relief that she no longer has to stand guard over my sister's virginity.

"Is she pregnant?" I ask.

Frowning, my sister mutters, "Very funny," and continues turning the pages of her magazine.

We're shivering in the kitchen of a damp cabin on a peninsula southwest of Seattle. Rain pummels the sides of the cabin as we clutch our hot cups of tea. A wooden sign with "Raven's Nest" in crudely engraved letters swings back and forth on a single rusty nail outside the front door. The waves thunder against the rocks below the bluff where the Raven's Nest is perched, holding what is left of my family within its four drafty walls.

"I didn't know you were seeing anyone," I stammer in Joanie's direction. My chest hurts, like when I was eight and got hit so hard by a wave it knocked the wind out of me.

Mother chatters about Joanie's fiancé ("He makes a good wage"), how the two met (at the rodeo), and wedding plans ("Burgundy and forest green are a nice combination for a December wedding, don't you think so, Catherine?").

Joanie gets up from her chair to straighten a laminated map of tsunami evacuation routes tacked to the kitchen wall. My mother reserved this cabin based on an ad that called it a "must-visit vacation getaway." The ad failed to mention that the cabin is over one hundred years old, is situated in one of the foggiest places in the country, two miles from Cape Disappointment, which boasts some of the most punishing currents seafarers have ever encountered.

In the four years I've been away from home and living in Seattle, this is the first time my mother and sister, who still live in the family house in eastern Washington, have come to visit me. But instead of my showing them around Seattle, they pick me up and we head straight to this cabin.

My sister Joanie graduated from high school in May. She had to give up her dream of qualifying for the Olympic gymnastics team after she suffered a severe back injury from a vault mishap. After she recuperated, she got a summer job working the concessions stand at the rodeo fairgrounds south of town.

According to my mother, that's where Joanie and Randy met and fell in love. Knowing nothing about rodeos, I imagine it went something like this: My sister hands the guy a rubbery hot dog and a plastic cup foaming over with Rainier beer. Randy removes the toothpick from his mouth, adjusts his Stetson to camouflage his receding hairline, and says, "Those ain't real diamonds, are they?" pointing to the studs in Joanie's ears, a high school graduation gift from Mother. And when Joanie answers, "Yes, yes they are," Randy takes a swig of beer, wipes his mustache on his sleeve, and offers, "Someday I'll give you a diamond you won't have to *squint* to see."

Wind whistles through the cracks in the Raven's Nest and daylight wanes. I ache to talk to Joanie alone, to have her make sense of this news for me. Growing up, she never expressed any interest in marriage or babies. As a teenager, she debated the issue with her girlfriends, equating marriage with paralysis. Her life vision was one of Olympic competition and travel. She had ambition and graduated high school a year earlier than most kids. Nothing seemed to deter her. Until her vault accident anyway.

Mother stops talking and applies "Mauve Haze" to her upper lip while straining in the fading light to see her reflection in a compact mirror. "This calls for a celebration!" she cries. "Let's drive into town for fisherman's stew."

Joanie and I look at each other. Joanie almost never feels like eating. She has subsisted for years, primarily on protein powder shakes, with her weight hovering around ninety-five pounds. Whenever she gained a pound or two (and she knew when that was because her coach submitted all his girls to weekly weigh-ins), she would immediately begin a grapefruit fast.

As for me, I gave up shellfish a couple of years ago to accommodate Ira, my Jewish psychiatrist boyfriend, who insists I maintain a kosher kitchen despite the fact we rarely eat dinner together.

But Mother is already wrapping a scarf around her head to hold her hair in place. The rain has slowed to a drizzle. We squeeze into the convertible my mother rented for the trip and head toward the only lights on the island. Water drips through a gap in the canvas car top and my right leg is soaked by the time we get to the restaurant.

The neon sign for Larry's Lobster Shack is missing a bulb under the "h" so that the sign blinks "Larry's Lobster Sack." A message written in magic marker on a piece of cardboard says: "You catch 'em, we'll cook 'em!" I wonder whether, being fishless, we'll be turned away.

Inside, two guys in flannel shirts are sitting at the bar, hunched over a cribbage board, with a pitcher of beer and a basket of fried oysters. The one with the curly white neck hair wipes his fingers on his trousers before making his move. The bartender lets out an "Oh, CHEE-sus!" in response to a football game he's watching on a nine-inch television tucked behind the bar. We wander over to a table in the corner by the window.

A waitress brings us water and menus and calls my mom "honey" even though she's half my mother's age. Joanie twists a strand of chestnut hair around her index finger while Mother reads the entire menu out loud.

Mom orders for all of us. When the food arrives, Joanie stares at the football game on the TV above my head. I shuffle the mussels and clams around in my bowl until a sea of garlicky stew splashes onto the red checkered tablecloth. Mother is drawing up a list of potential wedding guests. "If we invite the Pearsons," she says, "we'll have to include the Springers or we'll never hear the end of it. Dessert, you two?"

I stare out the window. I'm willing to accept anything in the way of meaningful form: the outline of a pelican, the movement of a fisherman's boat . . . but the world out there is unforgivingly gray-white, offering nothing in the way of a clear image and holding no promise for any indication of change.

That night I dream my sister is dying. My parents and I sit a polite distance from Joanie's hospital bed while Dad describes the camping trips we'll take together when Joanie is discharged. Mother keeps rearranging the flowers and get-well cards. We all smile and pretend Joanie is there for a routine tonsillectomy.

All weekend long, Mother blows a protective bubble around Joanie. Joanie, in turn, accepts this, never once expressing any feelings or opinions of her own about the wedding except to say she refuses to wear a garter.

I miss Ira. Despite the fact he and I are more like roommates than lovers right now, I long to be back in Seattle with him. I suspect he's cheating on me, but somehow this is more tolerable than being here in the Raven's Nest with my family.

***

The following week, I call home to Pullman. "Take the phone to your bedroom," I say when Joanie picks up. I don't want her responses tainted by Mother's hovering.

All day, I've rehearsed what I'm going to say. I'll tell her I think Randy is a lousy substitute for Olympic competition. I'll remind her that she's all of seventeen and that statistically she and Randy have less than a fifty percent chance of making it. I'll implore her to consider her options.

But when I hear her voice, I also hear us giggling on a summer's day long ago as I push her, all dressed up in doll clothes, in a crib around the neighborhood. "Don't leave me," I choke.

"Oh Cath," my little sister sighs, "we left each other a long time ago."

She says it in the same tone of voice she would use to say I have something stuck between my teeth. At first I think she is referring to my leaving home as soon as I graduated from high school. But instead she talks about the day of Daddy's funeral and how, from that point on, she and Mom and I treated each other like strangers.

It's true. After the funeral and the burial, after the last mourner left our house, Joanie went to the gym to practice her routine, Mother set about emptying ashtrays, and I escaped to my best friend's house where I slept for three days on the hide-a-bed in their TV room. My friend's mother made sympathetic noises while offering boxes of Kleenex and mugs of chamomile tea.

When I returned home, Mom, Joanie, and I settled into a form of polite cohabitation as if we were housemates who'd found each other through an ad in the newspaper. We got so used to living together in silence that when one of us spoke at the dinner table, it startled the other two, and all three of us would feel slightly rattled for the rest of the evening.

"Randy's my soul mate," Joanie says finally, and I realize our conversation is over.

My fingers are numb from gripping the receiver. It's past supper time. I picture Ira at a coffeehouse in the university district, some willowy, clove-cigarette-smoking graduate student cozying up to him. I grab my raincoat and head out.

At its best, September in Seattle delivers bright, still days with clear views of snowcapped Mount Rainier as a backdrop to the autumn camellias, blood-red kaffir lilies, and lacy-leaved Japanese maples. But this year, the rains returned in early September, and my visibility is reduced to one or two slabs of sidewalk as I cross Montlake Cut, heading toward campus.

Because it's dark by the time I reach the quad, I almost don't see her—an elderly woman wearing a plastic garbage bag as protection against the rain. She offers me a lily, petals drooping, and whispers what sounds like, "Beware of those you love." Her breath smells of tobacco and she's missing a couple of teeth. I wonder whether she has any family and where, or if, she sleeps at night. I think if I'm not more careful, I could end up like her—alone in the rain, with bad teeth.

***

The next morning Ira is gone when I wake up. A note he scribbled is taped to the espresso machine. "We need to talk," it says. I figure this'll be another one of those discussions where Ira insists we either get married or break up. And in the end, we do neither of those things. A few months will go by and we'll rehash the issue. It's what we do.

I call Nana, my father's mother, at her home in Seaside to ask if it's okay if I take the bus down to visit her for the weekend.

She's breathing hard when she picks up. "Okay, I'm sitting down," she shouts. "Who died?"

"No one died, Nana," I reassure her.

"Did you get expelled from school again?" she asks.

In the third grade I was suspended and given a heavy penance for pulling off Sister Teresa's veil to prove to my friend Linda that you really didn't have to shave your head to become a nun.

"No Nana. I'm in law school now," I say.

"I know that!" she snaps.

"Have you heard Joanie's getting married?" I ask.

"When I take you two girls to the candy shop," Nana starts (and I wonder which decade she's in now), "Joanie takes one look inside the glass and immediately points to a jar of root beer barrels. That girl knows what she wants! You, on the other hand, hem and haw as if which piece of candy you choose will determine your entire life's direction. You have such a gosh-darned time making up your mind."

It was, and still is, true. I live in that state of limitless possibilities even if it means going empty-handed in the end. It's the availability of choices that both fascinates and torments me.

The next morning I board a bus to Seaside. The bus smells of wet animal fur and whisky. Half-hour into the ride, I press my forehead on the cool glass of the window and try to see through the fog and sleet to the white line on the side of the road. Nauseated by the effort, I close my eyes.

The night my father died, he was parked at the top of a bluff east of town in that '67 Chevy he called his third kid. He wasn't alone.

They must have fallen asleep. Whether my dad forgot to set the parking brake or bumped it with his knee, or whether it was faulty or simply malfunctioned, we'll never know. It was one of many details the police failed to uncover about his, and his companion's, death.

A jogger found his car. My father's head was resting at an odd angle against the driver's seat window, his body slumped like a child's. The only thing separating my father's body from a hundred-year-old oak tree was the thin piece of metal the Chevy was reduced to. The body of his companion lay face down thirty feet away. The autopsy revealed both had died on impact. Both were "semi-clothed," according to the police report. Among the items found inside the car was a cooler filled with sandwiches, potato salad, and a six-pack of Rainier. AAA road maps showed a scenic route to New Mexico highlighted in yellow.

None of us, including my mother, cried at his funeral even though we had loved him very much. I think we were all too stunned to cry. Less stunned that his car went off the bluff than that he was leaving us for a total stranger. My sister, embarrassed about the circumstances of Dad's death, would tell new friends that our father died of lung cancer when she was a baby. It was an easier truth for her to tell.

In Seaside Nana greets my bus, holding a plastic flowered umbrella and wearing the kind of orthopedic shoes that only old people wear and a dress that looks exactly like the one she's wearing in photos of my baptism in 1957. As I nuzzle my face in the fleshy folds of her neck, I think, this is what happiness smells like—lavender rain and English Breakfast tea.

Nana slips her arm through mine and we walk quietly toward the beach past shops with marine-themed T-shirts hanging in the windows. When I was a kid, it was mostly the same families who came here every summer and the shops were geared toward their needs—a dime store with a great assortment of comic books, a hardware store, a candy shop where we could watch saltwater taffy being pulled, a bowling alley. Those stores have all been replaced by souvenir shops, deep-sea fishing outfitters, and bars that host wet T-shirt contests for college kids on spring break.

We walk along the beach without talking until the rain becomes more of a mist. Nana folds up her umbrella and I remove my hood. "You have your father's eyes," Nana observes.

I don't want to talk about Daddy, so I say, "For all her enthusiasm, you'd think it was Mother who's getting married."

"Well, that's understandable," Nana replies.

We scoot sideways to avoid snowy plovers scurrying about on toothpick legs.

"What do you mean?"

"Well, your mother always dreamed of a big Catholic wedding with bridesmaids, a full mass, the whole works."

It never occurred to me what sort of wedding Mom and Dad had. No wedding photos donned our walls or end tables as they did in our friends' homes. "What sort of wedding did they have?" I ask.

"Your parents were very much in love," Nana begins, "and you were very much wanted and loved and cared for as a baby. It's just that you came a little early."

"Early? As in premature? How early?"

"Well, they were married in late September 1956, and you came along the first day of spring."

The math comes easily and certain images rush to the forefront: the annoyed look on my mother's face when, as a little girl, I asked if I could play dress-up with her wedding dress. Mother screaming, "I won't have any pregnant teenagers in this household!" when I came home late from a date in high school. A wisecrack from my godfather making a toast at my parents' fifteenth wedding anniversary.

"Your mother never intended to marry so young," Nana continues. "Your father, on the other hand, was engaged to marry somebody else. Of course, he broke that off when your mother found she was expecting. Your father did the right thing by asking your mother to marry him."

"Why are you telling me this?"

"Because you have a right to know and because you'll never hear it from your mother."

We walk past signs prohibiting us from disturbing the shorebird nests in the sand dunes.

"Are you coming to the wedding?" I ask Nana.

"I'll be there with bells on," she says.

    ***

The day of my sister's wedding, in what would have been a lovely dress had someone else been wearing it, I arrive late to the church. I refused to attend a fitting at the dressmaker, so in addition to the dress being too tight, I discover that the scoop back makes wearing an ordinary bra difficult. I am bra-less, with a rip in my underarm, and the inside of my cheek keeps bleeding from my biting it.

Mother is wearing a billowy cream-colored creation that reminds me of Glinda, the Good Witch of the North. She floats from pew to pew welcoming guests. Anyone who doesn't know better might mistake her for the bride.

Nana is in the front pew, humming and tapping her fingers to the organ music. Occasionally she tugs on the ends of her wig, digs at her girdle, or twirls the thin gold band she wears constantly despite the fact my grandfather has been dead for over twenty years.

I decide I can't go through with this. I can't stand at the altar next to my sister and in front of her friends and our relatives and show support for this marriage. She's too young. Neither of them has a job. They've known each other for less than six months. They have no clear plan, no savings. They'll be divorced within a year.

I retreat to the bathroom and close myself in a stall. I cry that I'm losing my sister. I cry for having lost my father. I cry that my dress doesn't fit. When I'm done crying, I grab a wad of toilet tissue and blow my nose.

Joanie's dressing room is down the hall. I enter without knocking. She has a glass of champagne in one hand and a curling iron in the other.

I say, "If Dad were here . . ."

". . . he'd be griping about how much he had to shell out for a pair of tight slacks and a bolo tie," Joanie laughs.

"If Dad were here," I say, "he'd be smoking cigarettes in the alley with his buddies, taking bets on how long your marriage will last."

"If Dad were here," Joanie says, "he'd be reassuring his friends that when I get married the *second* time around, they won't have to buy me a gift!"

Outside the church window, the sleet is turning to snow and I think about the homeless woman on the quad. She didn't say, "*Beware.*" What she said was, "*Take care.*" Take care of the ones you love. And I know that whatever happens with Ira and me, it doesn't matter.

When my sister finishes with her hair, she slips her arm through mine and together we walk up the aisle. When we reach the altar, Joanie lets go of my arm and takes her fiancé's hand. I sit down next to Nana in the front pew and lay my head on her shoulder. She hands me a handkerchief with my father's initials on it. It smells of tobacco and cedar. The priest clears his throat and the ceremony begins.

Black Leather Jacket

Tim Calaway

(For Jean)

She comes in wearing the familiar black leather jacket
The one I've seen her wear so many times before
Nodding to the bartender he slides a beer her way
Probably a PBR or Miller Lite in a long-necked bottle
You know the kind you hold near the top
With your thumb and two fingers
So you can swing it towards those you know
As a way to say howdy across the room
She leans back into the wood of the friendly bar
Looks around and sees me and says
"When'd you get out of jail?"
She always says this to me as if I'm a repeat offender
I smile and say "Yesterday." She nods and looks up at the TV
Where a Pats game is playing
Boston strong, she bleeds Sox red, and Pats blue
Probably bleeds Celtic green too
I get up to leave and take one last look back
The familiar black leather jacket reflects neon
And the light from the fifty-inch screen.

Diablo Rojo

Brian Thedell

The midnight moonlight half against your cheek
Flickers with the glow against your hair from the nightlight...
The haze of the computer monitor—LCD...
Or maybe I'm thinking about the muted greys of a bar floor,
Or the blur of a midnight freeway beneath us...

The stain of solitude, the remote bedrooms of childhood and
The refuge of midnight offered awake beneath the sheet—
The walls stained black and white as the Christmas Eve "I Love Lucy"
Midnight Marathon begins the Candy Factory episode...

Midnight is the color of a drug deal, a blow job, a save game re-
loading again;
Midnight is the shape of a drunken night, or of a comedown
—because you lacked money, not nerve—midnight is the kingdom of all that
Should have been, but cannot be in daylight; midnight is the
silence of a secret,
Because that shade of him naked is too delicate to describe...

And midnight pushes against my neck with Doug's breath quicker,
then not at all—
It was the weight of midnight freed from my chest as he let me
finally go, I got up and his

Twin Siamese—eyes as neon blue as his—uncrossed a midnight
path…

And every downtown everywhere at midnight wears the
forgotten midnight party soundtrack
Of everyone who used to be there—midnight offers sanctuary,
harbors asylum
To every you you had to ditch at the club, and midnight reads just
like that letter I wrote
—and never sent—where I finally admit I was wrong to leave
him…

Midnight rages red and shock white as diablo rojo squid frenzy
Through prey, flicker a drowning technicolor murder; finally,
Still, midnight remains the color of longing for here in this hallway
between
Day and death, I always already wait for you, always already
wonder even
As you lie next to me, if the night air and the color of zero can
bring you back again
Tomorrow night, for the color and glow tonight is the same every
night until—maybe—
We're finally dead…

Enough of Death for Today

Diane Griggs

Darkness covers the earth, rain rides on the wind
& trees bend to peer through the window
as I sit & ponder Dante's Inferno.

Being a virtuous pagan maybe Virgil will assist
my navigation of these circles of suffering
permit me to reside in Limbo where I'll enter

the castle with seven gates & sit
at the feet of Homer, Horace & Ovid
as they recite their verses. Unless...

Minos, that judge of the dead, discovers
how I lusted after my neighbor's husband.
He, bare-chested, washing his red Porsche

in the driveway as I share my Dos Equis with him,
placing my lips where his have been, slipping
my tongue around the neck of the bottle.

I'll be banished to the second circle in the company
of Helen of Troy & Cleopatra, our souls blown
back & forth in a violent storm for eternity.

It's nearly dawn, already the sky studded with planes.

Joy of Man's Desiring

Sandy Robertson

Jocelyn had just returned to the shop with her lunch when the door swung open, setting all the little bells a-tinkle. She hurriedly stuffed the Big Mac, minus one bite, back into the paper bag, tucked the bag into the top drawer of the French Provincial desk and stood up with her most welcoming expression. "Good afternoon, Mr. Sterling," she said, careful to enunciate. "Welcome back to *Parfums de Plaisir*. How may I help you today?"

"Hello, Jennifer." He never got her name right, but what did it matter? She'd made it up anyway—Joyce was too pedestrian for an aspiring *parfumeuse*. Mr. Sterling sniffed the air appreciatively. "Smells good in here, is that some new perfume?"

Leaning forward, Jocelyn squeezed the drawer shut. "It could be, Mr. Sterling, it could well be. The latest arrival from Yves Saint Laurent is just in, if you'd like a sample?"

"Nah, that's okay. I'm here because, well, the Senator's wife's birthday is coming up, and he's asked me to pick up something for her."

"So, this would be for the wife, then." She kept her voice crisp and neutral, almost nonchalant.

"Yes, the wife, right. You know, like last time. Do you remember what it was he got her before? I guess she liked that, whatever it was."

Jocelyn hesitated. There was no choice. She had to open the drawer to get to her customer accounts. A distinct odor of hamburger and cheese escaped as she extracted the book, but her client seemed unperturbed. She squeezed the drawer shut again, smiling at him.

"I have on record that the Senator ordered a one-ounce flacon of Joy on December 22nd, two ounces of Dior's Hypnotic Poison on December 23rd, a special presentation bottle of Boucheron's Trouble, also on the 23rd, then Poivre by Caron on the first of January..."

Sterling interrupted. "Maybe that one. What's that one like?"

"A stirring fragrance, Poivre," said Jocelyn. "A blend of red and black pepper, with a dash of ylang-ylang...."

"Sounds like Worcestershire sauce to me," said Sterling, and laughed. When Jocelyn didn't join in, he offered, "Like for hamburger?"

Jocelyn returned a perfected expression of bewilderment, eyebrows raised. "Beg your pardon?"

Sterling sighed and looked down at the accounts book. "Which one costs the most? That'd be the one for the wife, don't you think?"

"Yes, of course, very good. Let's see," Jocelyn said, bending to her book. "That would be the Joy, at $850 an ounce."

"Okay, good enough," said Sterling, nodding. "I think that's it. Joy. Damn, I wish the Senator would keep a list of what goes where." He scratched his ear. "Guess maybe as Chief of Staff I'm the one who should undertake that." He glanced at Jocelyn, who continued peering at her book.

"Indeed, there's one other possibility," she murmured, marking the page with a lacquered red fingernail. "Perhaps this is the one the Senator intended for his wife? Chanel No. 5. Per ounce, of course, it's not as expensive as Joy. But it shows here that the State of Delaware paid $1,950 for a fifteen-ounce crystal bottle last September 9th. Would that be the wife's birthday?"

The Chief of Staff and Jocelyn gazed at each other.

"No, that must've been something else. The wife's birthday is tomorrow."

"I see," said Jocelyn. She looked down at the book again.

"Hmm. Well, perhaps it is the Joy then. One ounce? Shall I gift wrap it for you?"

"Yes, please. Thanks, Jennifer. Oh, and can you make out a card for the Senator to sign?"

"Certainly, *avec plaisir.*"

Sterling took the package, smiled wanly, and left the shop, bells tinkling.

***

Mid-morning three weeks later Mr. Sterling reappeared. This time the shop smelled of bergamot and sandalwood. Jocelyn had taken to eating green salads for lunch in order to guarantee the appropriate atmosphere at all times. The effect was lost on Mr. Sterling, however.

Jocelyn stood to greet him. "Good day, Mr. Sterling. Very nice to see you again. What may I do for you?"

"Nice to see you too, Jennifer. I'm, uh, afraid I'm going to need your help. There's been a bit of a problem."

"A problem?" Jocelyn smoothed her skirt. "Of course. I'll help in any way I can."

"You see, the Senator's wife dropped by the office the other day, and, well, it seems the Senator's executive assistant was wearing Joy when she served the wife coffee."

"Ah," said Jocelyn.

"There was quite a tussle. The Senator's wife broke her wrist in the ensuing, what would you call it...*mêlée.*"

"Ah, yes. Altogether understandable, though regrettable."

"The Senator's wife was, well, extremely upset. She, uh, laid down an ultimatum, you might say."

Jocelyn measured her words. "I see. So, I would imagine, you'll not be placing any further orders for Joy."

"That's correct. No more Joy."

"Very good, Mr. Sterling. I assure you I will strike every instance of Joy from the Delaware accounts." She lifted her chin. "Need I be concerned with the remaining orders?"

"Well, no, not now. You see, the Senator's wife already knew about the other orders, even the Chanel No. 5, apparently. Not that she was happy about any of it, God knows, but it was the duplication of Joy that flipped her, since she thought the Joy was reserved only for her. So, now, this brings up another matter where I need your help, if possible—related to the first."

"Of course, by all means."

"No more Joy for the Senator's wife, but in its place, she wants a perfume that you haven't sold to anyone, anytime, anywhere. Ever." Sterling stared at Jocelyn in dismay. "Is that even possible?"

Jocelyn drew a small, quick breath and straightened her spine. "Certainly possible, Mr. Sterling. Absolutely." Thoughts racing, she smiled at him. "Indeed, why not? What woman in Washington would wear a dress worn by another to the Inaugural Ball? It's unthinkable."

"The wife's dead serious. She swears she's going to notify *The Washington Post* of all the perfume accounts if the Senator fails to meet her demands. Meaning, this could be it, Jennifer. For the Senator, and, of course, for me." He looked away.

"How much time do we have, Mr. Sterling?" Jocelyn smiled. A bright future was unfolding before her. She imagined her business card. "A moment, please—I will do an estimate," she said. She picked up a notepad and half-turned from him, scribbling:

Parfum à Votre Caprice
Mme. Jocelyn Prudent
Owner, Fragrance Designer
Personalized Perfume for the Truly Unique Woman:
Never Duplicated, Never Forgotten, Never Replaced

She faced him, her gaze steady. *"Oui, bien sûr.* I can create a perfume for the Senator's wife," she said. "And for her alone. Naturally it will take several sessions to find the perfect blend, a pure and concentrated essence that distinguishes the wife among all others. I will make enough to keep in stock for her; then I will destroy the formula. It will be unavailable to anyone else. Promise her that."

"Wonderful, that's just wonderful, Jennifer. Whatever you need to carry this out, you have it. The Senator will back you one hundred percent, you can count on it. Whatever you need." Sterling was smiling from ear to ear.

"I will need five or six months," Jocelyn said evenly, "and ninety-seven thousand dollars."

"No problem, you got it, Jennifer. You have no idea how happy we are to oblige. I'll tell the Senator's wife to call you for an appointment right away. Just send us the bill."

"So I shall," said Jocelyn, tilting her head to hide her excitement. "And by 'us,' do you mean you and the Senator? Or should I bill the State of Delaware?"

"It's one and the same, honey, one and the same."

Bird On It

Catherine Darby

Birdsongs woke us,
different trumpet
calls carried their way
through tent walls,
I chirped your chest
you whistled my breast
I caw your thigh
under coverlet,
you stole my coo.
Bellows twist and ruffle,
humming chirps chatter
with quaver kisses,
through restless tongues and
deep breaths. We warble.

Fly Girl and the Spider

Diane Malloy

This guy wasn't the type I normally went out with—since inter-species dating wasn't really my thing.

But hey, I'd been jilted by enough bug-eyed sweet-talkers, who were always taking off, ready for something new.

My last boyfriend, Zzzack, would take me out to the dumpster for a "special" meal. But, did he really think I couldn't see him rubbing his legs in the direction of the other girls? Giving them the eye?

The last straw was when I caught him with Betzzy from next door, cavorting on a scoop of ice cream from that little human's cone.

Hello? Had he forgotten that these 4,000 lenses don't miss much? That I can pretty much see, three-hundred-and-sixty degrees? Heck, even if I wanted to, I couldn't look away. And believe me, watching them smear melted strawberry goop on each other, I wanted to.

So there I was, buzzing around the kitchen, alone again on a Friday afternoon, avoiding the occasional magazine swat, when I saw this cute guy hanging in the corner of the ceiling. Watching me. I took a couple of laps around the leftover pizza on the kitchen table, then landed on the ceiling near him.

He yelled, "Hey, gorgeous! You've got the most beautiful eyes. How come I haven't seen you here before?"

I tilted my head and twitched. Then while he watched, I took a leisurely spin around the room to show off my shimmering, iridescent wings. When I landed on the ceiling light, he scurried over.

"What's a knockout like you doing hanging around the kitchen?" He looked me over. "With a thorax like that, you could go places."

I smiled and brushed my antennae, but couldn't look away from his shiny black eyes.

His mouth curved. "How's about coming over to my place tonight? Maybe have a quick bite?"

Inside, I was buzzing. He looked good, like he watched what he ate.

"What time?"

"7:00? I live under the porch, next to the top stair."

"Okay. See you then."

After he crawled away, I swooped to the bathroom sink and washed my face in a drop of water, licked at a splash of mouthwash, and shook out my wings. Then I took a little siesta behind the living room drapes.

Ready at 7:00, I flew out an open window, found the porch stair and glided beneath it.

My strapping suitor beamed at me from the a bed of silky strands. His eyes glinted. "I did this all for you, baby," he said in a voice low and seductive.

"For me? Oh...it's breathtaking!" I moved towards him, then hesitated, "So...dinner?"

His eyes narrowed. "Yeah, you are."

"Excuse me?"

His jaw opened wide. I tried to step back, but my feet were stuck!

He lunged towards me, but I twisted and kicked and somehow got free, just as his teeth grazed my wing.

I panicked and flew in circles, faster and faster, looking for a way out. Heard his jaw snapping.

Then, there it was... an opening! The humans had turned on their porch light and I zoomed towards it. My injured wing burned, but I was free.

Later in the kitchen, I landed on my dinner: pizza for one. And it had never tasted so good.

Diet Craze

Cherie Kephart

No more excuses. No more second, third, or fourth thoughts. She walked toward him, his head like a pineapple, rough and spiky but sweet on the inside. Her cannibalistic urge to cut it open, to see if it was ripe, was strong, saliva-producing strong. But he didn't deserve it. Or did he?

Those moments of sanity hurled in between her latest lunacy kept her away from the extra-sharp knife set she had bought late Saturday night on QVC, not to be confused with the extra-sharp imported provolone cheese she purchased last Tuesday on formaggio.com.

Bananas! She was going bananas! You peel them, no blades necessary. Another yellow fruit, not as juicy as pineapple, but it would do.

She munched on the gooey pieces of gorilla grub and watched him read the newspaper, lounging in his easy chair drinking Lucky Lager and eating Slim Jims, as if he owned the world and was checking on the status of his investment. "Slim Jims!" she thought, "there is nothing slim about him, and his name isn't, well, wait, his name is James, but NOT Jim."

Somehow his body looked different. She noticed it more now than ever during their two decades together; the copious contours, the bountiful brown blades of hair covering his arms and legs. His midsection resembled an upside-down pear jammed into jeans.

She caught herself daydreaming. "Jam. I simply cannot resist huckleberry preserves. I should make some this year." No! No more time to play Martha Stewart, although prison would be next if she followed through with her plan. Not necessarily. She recalled hearing of a Twinkie Plea, but she didn't have any Twinkies. She wondered, "Would the judicial system accept a Ding Dong plea?" A whole new meaning to *death by chocolate*.

She stepped closer to him; her noodles for arms swayed while her oatmeal-textured thighs jiggled. "Oat-meal. How can oats be a meal? You at least need nuts on top."

She was nuts all right, the mixed-variety kind, salted and rancid. She could feel the madness moving through her blood. The corners of her mouth turned upward, ever so slightly.

"What's wrong with me?" She hated rhetorical questions, especially when she asked them of herself. She knew what was wrong. It was that rotten piece of turkey over there in the recliner, marinating in his ninety-nine-cent cologne that smelled one chemical compound shy of formaldehyde.

Her stomach growled. She didn't know how she would accomplish "the act." All she was armed with was her Guns and Roses *Appetite for Destruction*. "Step aside Axl, here I come." Wait, that's it! She would use an axe! Only, she didn't have one. Damn suburban living.

The preliminary foul play made her thirsty. She grabbed her water bottle and guzzled like she had just crossed the Mojave Desert, not to be confused with dessert, which she could easily do. Only one little letter.

Ah, tiramisu, her favorite. She wasn't certain what ladyfingers were, and how the Italians incorporated even more cheese, the lovely mascarpone, into the sweet section of their cuisine, but they did. She craved that sugary goodness, but all she had were bitter cravings directed toward What's-His-Face.

Hang on. She couldn't even remember his name. She glared at him. He looked like no one she recognized, an assortment of shapes, colors, and odors molded together into a nebulous blob of Jell-O.

Would this make it easier? Not remembering his name? That

could come in handy. Add it to the Ding Dong plea. More and more she had a defense, her actions fueled by an insatiable hunger for human carnage. "He might even taste like chicken."

She could taste the deed. She scurried to the kitchen. He paid no attention, his eyes still glued to the printed pages full of thousands of squiggles, like tiny pieces of black licorice.

She passed the opened pantry. Shelves of packaged foods with long lists of ingredients, which took several attempts and a dictionary to pronounce, glowered at her. She jumped back, startled by the bright labels adorned with festive logos, all showcasing their newest *natural* artificial flavor. From the top shelf, the Hamburger Helper grinned, egging her on.

"Do it now!" her stomach wailed. She collapsed onto the floor, sobbing. "I can't take it anymore!"

A thin, long ray of sunlight flickered a few feet from her, like a stream of golden caramel. She traced the light to the window above the sink and spotted several giant marshmallows floating across the sky.

She crawled over to the shiny knife set adjacent to the cookie jar lined with crumbs and the never-used Jack LaLanne Juicer. She stood up, erect like a stalk of asparagus, and grabbed the largest blade in the block. Her attention shifted to the refrigerator; the shimmering stainless steel beckoned. She clenched the knife and opened the door.

The metallic giant was chock full of FDA barely-approved consumables. The hefty amount of unnatural colors and forms of fodder filling the belly of the beast shocked her. "Junk!" she shouted, "It's all refuse! There are no neon green nutrients! And since when do cows produce orange cheese?"

In a flash, her outlandish hankering for homicide extinguished. It wasn't his fault, it was them! She placed the knife on the counter. All along she had been duped by the sweet-as-pie diet and food industry. They did this to her!

Her diet was driving her insane! She was starved for chow that nourished, not created addiction. He was simply the stooge, unaware of his role in abetting her dependence on these products.

"No more diets! I'm finished!" A wave of calm surged through her.

From across the house, a voice shouted, "Hey honey, a package came for you, it's from ThinNow Inc. And oh, what's for dinner?"

Her pupils dilated. Her neck stiffened. She walked over to the knife, picked it up and stroked the glistening blade. In a smooth and syrupy voice she called back, "Pineapple."

Love Lost

Jay M. Mower

She flies into a Vesuvian rage so quickly
I don't even recall what unleashed
the molten lava, but SLAM! SLAM! SLAM!
reverberates down the corridor
and an emptiness prisms hallway walls
from a summer hue to shades of lonesome blue.

Walking inside the darkening atrium,
I realize she's blazing bananas.
By the time I climb into my car,
I'm convinced she's *cucuzza* crazy.
My fantasy, *she'll soon be sorry.*

I toss her photo down the garbage chute
and mulch reappears… throw her name
into the recycling bin, but she comes back
as plastic wrap. Frantic, I mail her love
in a hate letter that returns postage due,
so I hurl her from Mount Quandary,
but she flows back as a gentle breeze.

Alone in myself, I miss gentle strokes
of her hand, the radiance of her laugh
and a wisp of her *Chanel.* She chases me
down the avenues, pulls me back

with gentle tugs and slithers into my mind
whether I'm gaming, preparing bids
or savoring backyard barbecued ribs.

TV tray after TV tray of silence penetrates
my mares-nest mind, loneliness screams
that her love will not return to me
on a simple spin of fortune's whim.

An Unbidden Guest

Ellen Yaffa

S he reveals herself bit by bit, progressing like the phases of the moon. As a nascent sliver she may make you wait an hour or two to doze into a decent slumber. By the end, you greet the morning sun as though you had pushed the moon through its entire cycle all by yourself, sweating from the exertion and slamming its perfect round orb into the rising sun, exclaiming, "Thank God *you're* finally here."

InSomnia is a demon who moves in under cover and then overstays like an unbidden guest. At first her suitcase appears all on its own, without her, but you know it's hers because you suddenly feel wide awake at 10:30 p.m. after being exhausted all evening. You have come to recognize her luggage tag and her scent, and so you make stealth preparations so as to not fully acknowledge and thus mistakenly welcome her arrival. You casually begin the bedtime rituals—aware you are not noticing the luggage, forcing an upbeat lightness as the electric Sonicare whizzes around your molars and the anti-aging night cream gives your face a dewy glow. You fluff the pillows, put on the ocean sound CD and start to read. You choose short stories or *New Yorker* articles that can be finished within fifteen minutes, sleep prompts as it were. Personal narrative or witty fiction, nothing too serious or angst-provoking like the creeping terror of ISIS or how inmates languish in prison because they cannot make bail.

The following evening, InSomnia herself shows up perched on a crescent, filing her nails and popping gum. "Hi chump," she says, "what are we gonna do tonight?" The little shit is a big nocturnal conversationalist, like a bat with vocal chords.

"I'm brewing herbal tea," you reply, "Celestial Seasonings Sleepytime Extra. Why don't we wash down a melatonin with it? And by the way, you don't scare me, I am not stressing. I'll be resting peacefully while you, you restless hussy, make me tug at the covers and change positions every five minutes." She snaps her gum just as Deepak Chopra is telling us to concentrate on our breath, in and out, in and out.

Now that the cycle is officially underway, the pace accelerates. You bring the print New York Times to bed, which during the day, on the couch, is a certain soporific. You finish the Book Review, even the ads, but no nodding occurs. Maybe the David Foster Wallace book, exhausting with all those damn footnotes. This is the phase, about three-quarters into the cycle, in which InSomnia lets you fall asleep after an hour or two of position changes, self-coached breathing (in, out, in, out) and alphabet light. Alphabet light is when you challenge yourself to name at least one city and country for each letter of the alphabet and are thrilled when you realize you must have dozed off because you can't remember if you are on M or R.

Of course InSomnia is not finished with you yet. Like the song says, "Without you pushing it the tide rolls in…" You step it up to Tylenol PM (wuss that you are, you take only a half dose), washed down with more Sleepytime Extra tea. You know the bitch has unpacked and moved in. Pretty soon she'll float away like Mary Poppins, but you're in full moon mode now for a night or two. You are no longer playing alphabet light; you progress to more difficult categories such as names of artists and authors, starting and stopping with winks and nods—I, P, even Z. You call out to your talking digital clock to find out the time without opening your eyes. "Hello Moshi!" you say, the only words to which the robot will respond. "Command, please," she replies. "Time," you cue. Hallelujah! Two hours have passed since the last check-in, and you realize at that instant that you and breastfeeding infants are on the same sleep cycle. You search for the sweet spot on the mattress like the Princess and the Pea, change pillows, do a yoga meditation and turn totally around, pointing your feet towards the headboard.

After all this activity, it's 2:30 a.m. You roam the house like Lady Macbeth. Read *The Week* magazine in the living room. Flip on the TV. Field the litany of nagging questions that appear like a receiving line: Do you have enough money to last the rest of your life? What if the damn condo never sells? Is that a bug bite on your neck or a cancerous lymph node? Did your grandson get a meningitis booster? Will your son get captured while on assignment in Eastern Ukraine? The anxieties greet you one by one, exiting with a toothy, gum-exposed grin, "Nite-nite, toots, sleep tight."

The kicker, of course, is the angst deriving from the problem itself: You read. You watch TV. You have learned how important sleep is; six to eight good hours hold the keys to the kingdom of good health. You want those keys. "What kind of cruel catch 22 is this?" you ask Moshi (the clock that cannot answer). Someone who can't get to sleep or stay asleep is bombarded by cheery, luminous faces cooing how restful sleep is the only thing between you and severe depression.

By 4:00 a.m. you return to bed, aggressively shoving InSomnia onto the floor. You sleep. And then, when the sky is a perfect paintbox Southern California blue, and the birds are chirping, and your neighbors are getting their newspapers off their front porch without having been frontline troops on duty all night long, you awaken for the day with a spring in your step.

Because the cycle is complete. InSomnia poses no more threat to you for the next few weeks than the man in the moon.

Lucy

Jill Murray

(from *Everything Crooked*)

I pulled on the heavy glass door at the Constitution Avenue entrance to the Smithsonian Natural History Museum and shuffled through security screening. The guard poked his baton in my Army surplus backpack, nudging aside my notebooks and a bag of Twizzlers. I offered him one, but he glanced up only long enough to wave me through. I grabbed my pack and made my escape into the museum. Pausing to orient myself, I scanned for a directory. I picked my way through the crowd and approached the information desk near the escalators.

"Where is the section on ancient humans?" I asked the uniformed woman. Seated, she could barely see over the top of the counter.

Without looking at me, she pointed to the escalator to my right and said, "First floor. Through Ocean Hall. Keep going through the Time Portal."

My heart thumped with unexpected anxiety. My lungs tightened and my shortened breaths were raspy. "Time Portal?"

The uniformed woman finally made eye contact, her expression quizzical. "Yeah, it's basically a hallway between the exhibits."

"Oh." I grinned a goofy smile and chuckled at my reaction for her benefit. I was glad she couldn't read my mind as I recalled the events of my last time slippage.

She looked like she'd had her fill of crazy tourists. Her face returned to its previous blankness.

The terse directions sent me on a winding course through the ocean exhibit. Museum designers surely had the same training as department store designers. There was no direct route to anything. In order to arrive at my destination, the layout forced me to pass by exhibits that were of no interest to me, although the size of that squid did make me pause.

I was glad to emerge from Ocean Hall. It had been filled with gangs of elementary school kids on a field trip. Their hyperactivity as they ran from one glass case to the next had me gritting my teeth. If I heard one more kid shriek at first sight of the whale, I thought I might scream myself.

The Time Portal to the Human Origins exhibit was built onto a generic hallway, with surfaces rounded to mimic a tunnel. The walls displayed images of some early hominins, but I kept walking without reading any of the captions. Long strips of blue neon lighting glowed on the ceiling, I suppose to create an atmosphere of time travel. I shook my head at how far it was from my experience.

There she was to the right, in a glass-enclosed diorama. Lucy, *Australopithecus afarensis*, the subject of next week's post on my blog, *Time Shadows*. Lucy's left foot was solidly on the ground, her left arm by her side. She stepped up on a rock at the base of a tree with her right foot and, with her right hand, she grasped the V of the tree trunk. Lucy, at least the Smithsonian's version of her, gazed to the left, perhaps at others of her group or perhaps at the rustling grass that might hide a predator. Her body, covered in fur, looked more primate than human.

Fascinating to think she was an ancestor.

I sniffed the air. My stomach grumbled and the aroma of popcorn made me aware I was hungry. I wondered where it came from; no one near me seemed to have any. It was definitely popcorn though. I could smell the butter combined with the faint whiffs of burnt kernels.

The intense odor worried me, since the acuity of my senses always increased before a slippage. High-pitched shrieks from the school children echoed in the tunnel behind me. As each voice joined the cacophony, it felt like a bolt of electricity went through my head. The light in Lucy's display flickered twice, then the case went dark.

I had to get away from the screaming. Looking to my left, I saw a museum employee open a locked door and enter the staff area. I jogged to the door and caught it with my fingers before it closed. I waited a moment, glanced over my shoulder to be sure no one noticed, and I stepped inside a dim stairwell. I sat down, covering my head with my arms to stave off further sensory input.

***

The feeling that someone was stabbing me in the head with scissors had stopped, but I kept my eyes closed. I felt a cool breeze brush across my face. The air smelled of moss and rotting leaves, of the forest. I heard water rippling nearby. I inhaled deeply.

I sat on the ground beneath a tree canopy at the edge of a stream. I let my eyes adjust and readied myself for the inevitable exploration that came with a slippage. I licked my lips and realized I was thirsty. I'd never consumed anything during a slippage before, but my mouth was so dry and the water so clear and inviting, I cupped my hands in the water and raised them to my mouth.

Bliss. I never knew water could taste so good when it had no taste. No taste of chemicals or who knows what impurities. It was cool and crisp, slippery and clean, and it quenched my thirst unlike anything else I ever had. I'd never eaten or drunk anything during earlier slippages, so it came as a complete surprise.

In front of me was vast grassland like I'd seen in African safari photos. I stepped into the open. I watched a cloud of dust moving along the horizon. After a few minutes it veered toward me and as it got closer I could see it was a herd of elephants. Or animals that looked like elephants. I glanced back at the tree line just as a lion jumped down from its perch and loped toward the oncoming herd.

Blocking the harsh sunlight with my hand, I gazed out over the savanna. A column of smoke burst from the top of a mountain in the middle distance. The ground trembled. Birds flew up from the grassland, racing to the forest where I had been minutes ago. I watched, frozen in place, as fire and rock and ash shot into the sky. Hot, red lava poured down the side of the volcano. As the clouds of ash lifted and caught the breeze, I came to my senses and jogged toward the woods in search of cover. Hundreds of rodent-like creatures raced around me into the trees.

Monkeys chattered above me as I reached the forest. My toe caught on a tree root and I fell to my palms and knees. Soon the dense ash cloud would reach me. I saw a rock jutting from the side of a small incline and ran to it for shelter. There was a hollow log nearby and I scraped out the moss and leaves to create more space. I dragged the log further under the overhang and, hoping there were no poisonous insects or plants to deal with, climbed inside.

I attempted to calm my breathing as I listened to the sounds of who-knows-what kind of animals running past my hiding place. No living thing had ever interacted with me during a slippage. I crossed my fingers that it would be no different this time. Some of the ash drifted through the trees and into my tiny log cabin. I tugged my shirt over my nose and mouth and was grateful it was sufficient to filter the ash.

I waited for the expected drowsiness that would return me home, but even as the sounds of the animals faded, I remained entirely alert. Ash continued to fall so I kept under cover. I don't know how long I waited, but it was into the next day, sufficiently long to be grateful I never experienced hunger during slippages. I wondered why I had encountered no people yet. Mid-morning, a light rain began to fall and the air cleared enough for me to explore again.

I hiked downstream and, having acquired a walking stick, poked the thick ash on the ground to identify any unstable terrain. As the stream began to seem more like a river and the trees thickened along the banks, a clearing opened and I had a view into the distance. Rising up at the far edge of the field was a large silver ovoid structure, entirely unfamiliar to me. I thought I heard voices in the distance so I inched closer in an attempt to hear what was being said.

A door or window, something, opened on the side facing me. Two creatures guided cages down a ramp. They were human-like, but not human, and spoke to each other with sounds that were more like clicking noises. Their proportions were off; the arms and legs were too long and slender. Their movements were too fluid, as if they had no joints, or even bones for that matter. But they had heads and faces, hands and feet, fingers and toes. They wore tunics over skirts that came to their ankles. They wore no shoes.

When the rolling cages came to a stop at the bottom of the ramp, where two more of these creatures waited, the bars raised and five apes scrambled out onto the ground, wailing in apparent fear. The cages were rolled back up the ramp into the structure, the four strange creatures following inside. The opening closed seamlessly. The apes, now cowering, hadn't moved from their original location.

The structure rose up on stilts and I realized it was a rocket of some kind, but not like anything NASA had ever launched. Grooves appeared on the exterior and began to twist. As the speed increased, the grooves blurred and then, with no more noise than a strong gust of wind, the ship was gone.

After a few moments, the apes stood erect, so not apes at all. With short humanoid gaits, two began to cross the clearing, their clear footprints imprinted the ash, wet from the morning shower. I followed them, stepping carefully in the tracks of the one on the right.

As they reached a tree, one placed its hand into the V of the trunk and turned to the left, towards me. Our eyes locked. Her stare penetrated to my core, to my very DNA.

Lucy.

The two creatures then continued into the woods and I stopped at the tree to rest. I yawned, an indication I'd be returning to my present day life soon. I sat on a rock and leaned against the gnarly tree trunk.

***

I awoke in the stairwell and shivered at the temperature change, so cool compared to the African climate I'd slipped to. When I opened the door to re-enter the Human Origins exhibit, I saw a museum docent finishing her comments about Lucy. As she led the school children past the display of fossilized footprints, I overheard her.

"Notice the slight deformation of footprints on the right. Some scientists have speculated the tracks of this *Australopithecus afarensis* were distorted perhaps because it carried an infant or child, thus altering the weight distribution."

The children drew close to the image to examine the human-like tracks.

"Others have said it's possible a third *Australopithecus afarensis* followed by stepping nearly directly in the footprints of another. It's something we will never know."

But I knew. As the group moved on, I discreetly removed one of my shoes and held my bare foot against the image. I chuckled with the awareness that the image most certainly was not life-size, despite what the description said.

Hadewig Stylites

Jan Thompson

It's 5:35 p.m. and Lili Marlene still isn't home from the grocery shopping. She's buying his booze, too, which is more to the point. MacArthur rolls his chair to the picture window in the living room and watches the snow pelting down at an angle in the street lights. Normally, they would be doing this together. They wait for it, without saying it, all year long; have done so since they were little. It's only special right before Christmas. Afterwards, it's depressing.

Weird how things change from magical to soul-sucking in the blink of an eye. Particularly true about everything having to do with Christmas, he reflects.

Pain gnaws its way up his spine. Most likely it's the cancer cells doing their thing as they always do when he's got a hangover. He fishes an OxyContin out of his robe pocket and crunches it down dry. It's not nearly as good as booze. Aquavit, eau de vie, uisge, the waters of life. Oh how he craves a cold, rummy eggnog.

Once he's wasted, he can sit and stare out the window at the Vest's Christmas lights. Red, blue, green, red, blue, green until the universe runs out of gas! Nothing can touch him then.

Where in the hell is Lili Marlene? There isn't a drop in the house. He knows, because he already crawled down the kitchen steps into the garage on his hands and knees and checked all the cupboards where she hides the booze from him.

Her cat Fluffy is up on the table eating his lunch. He throws his slipper at her but she keeps at it. Did she forget to feed her damned cat?

A note is stuck under the soup bowl. It's how she communicates when he's in a foul mood. Her predictability drives him mad and she isn't even in the house.

December 22, 2013   Jesus, Mary and Joseph
Dear MacArthur,

You told me last night that you're not a good person. That isn't true. Remember when we were going to Our Lady of the Most Blessed Sacrament—when I was in eighth grade and you were in sixth—and I put on lipstick and eye shadow and the kids made fun of me? Gemma Nardozzi said my eyebrows grew together in the middle and my legs were built like stumps. My parents must have been blind and crazy to name me after a beautiful woman.

You hit her on the head with your catechism and told her she had a butt like a B-52. You shouldn't have done those things, but I appreciated the gesture.

You always watched out for me, MacArthur. You will always be my little brother. Remember what Mom said right before she passed. We only have each other and we must stick together to the end. I hope you remember that in case I decide to do something really stupid again.

XoXo
Lili Marlene

PS We will be reborn in the blood of Our Lord and Savior, and warmed by the love of his Holy Mother. We can pretend to each other, MacArthur, but not to them. In heaven, there is only love and it burns like a fire.

MacArthur reads the note twice, turns it over and examines the back.

There's a loud rapping on the front door. It's the littlest Vest kid. Lili Marlene usually deals with the neighbors. He opens the door a crack. The kid shoves three UPS boxes into MacArthur's lap. More of her eBay crap. Even the boxes look like they've been used over and over. Damn. More shite to add to the rest of the claptrap in her bedroom and closet. He starts closing the door.

"Mr. Chizek, Mom says you need to turn on the news. Your sister's on TV. Mom says you can call her if you need any help."

His heart thuds and skips. The crash, it's finally come. Blood and carrots in the slush, Lili Marlene's head protruding from the windshield, his booze trickling down the trunk. He jabs the remote through all the channels.

The headline runs along the bottom of the TV, "Local woman climbs billboard outside state package store, resists rescue efforts of Mesquatine Fire Department and police. Story at 6."

What the F? This can't be his sister. Then he sees the fur-trimmed galoshes dangling over the side of the platform, kicking back and forth. He smacks his forehead with his palm.

There they are, for the whole world to see, to fleer and scorn. Every year she wears them at Christmas, every year he mocks and torments her about the way they gape and squish, the way she's bringing shame upon the entire family, living and dead, by wearing them in public. To no avail.

He rolls his chair back and forth in front of the window, creasing the cover of one of his old chemical engineering journals under the wheels. He spots her cell phone on the counter. She forgot it, again. He tears his hair.

He could call a cab, he supposes. He'll never ask the neighbors for help.

God, what if she died up there on the platform, or fell off?

What if she went around the bend and had to be institutionalized?

Who would take care of him? Who would buy him booze and hide it from him?

***

Lili Marlene is closing the trunk when she spots something luminescent moving around above her. She's right underneath the billboard. It's always displayed ads for the Wolf Creek Baptist Church, with big crosses, praying hands and Biblical passages.

Maybe they're doing something flashy for Christmas. It's one of those fancy animated signs, a meadow sprinkled with wildflowers, a plashing brook, puffy clouds moving across a bright blue sky, butterflies and twittering birds somersaulting through the air. Scents of roses and jasmine and new mown hay drift down to her as she stands in the frozen parking lot, and her hair curls in the warm, humid breeze.

Wait, how can this be?

She's thunderstruck. A radiant young woman in a long gown leads a naked baby boy through the grass. He toddles, looks up at his mother and laughs, baring two little teeth. The lady looks up and sees Lili Marlene for the first time. She smiles at her, a radiant smile filled with love. Lili Marlene hasn't been loved since Mom died five years before, and this is love multiplied a hundred times, a million times.

Her eyes fill with tears of happiness. She falls on her knees and clasps her hands, never taking her eyes off the beautiful lady and her sweet baby.

Then he beckons with a rosy hand. Lili Marlene climbs the ladder propped against the platform. She climbs more nimbly than she has in years. Mom's galoshes are as light as the wings of a dragonfly. She dances on tiptoe through juicy green grasses, sits down at the feet of the lady and clasps her knees. They're surrounded by golden light.

The lady hands her the baby. Lili Marlene kisses him again and again, hugs him tenderly. He wraps his arms around her neck and kisses her cheeks. Her soul overflows.

"Henceforth you will be Hadewig, Hadewig Stylites. You are the Blessed anchorite who climbs the ladder to adore My Son. You will remember why He was born, and how much He suffered for His love. You will remember He is an endless ocean of love, and I am the Star of the Sea."

Much more she says, speaking directly to Lili Marlene's

(Hadewig's) heart and soul. They talk about galoshes, mothers and brothers, recipes for cooking fresh fish. Our Lady unbends; they shed tears over Her Son's fate while He plays happily in the grass, unaware.

That's how they find her, on the top of the billboard platform, engaged in an animated conversation with no one. Next to her is an open can of adhesive, a paint brush and a large tube containing a printed ad for the Wolf Creek Baptist Church.

One of her former catechism students, Ervin Novotny, a volunteer fireman, climbs the ladder to bring her down. His chief, Randy Boldt, a man who went to school with her fifty years ago, climbs up after him. Then a young newcomer climbs up after him. So there are three big firemen on the platform and Lili Marlene (Hadewig).

"We know her," says the chief, smirking, to the newcomer. "It's Lili Marlene...Chizek," he chortles. The newcomer looks at him blankly. Lili Marlene (Hadewig) smiles. The new generation knows nothing about the lascivious old song.

Lili Marlene (Hadewig) refuses to budge. They coax, cajole, reminisce about old times, discuss the priest who was fired for child molestation, the Kansas City Chiefs and the flooding of the Mississippi River the previous spring. Everything but her vision.

A news crew from the local TV station shows up with microphones and cameras, yells questions. Lili Marlene (Hadewig) raises her hands and everyone falls silent.

"In three days we will celebrate the birth of Christ Our Lord. He was born to save us all when we had gone astray. Let's remember the death He died. And His Mother, the Blessed Virgin, who watched in agony as Her Son sacrificed Himself so man may live forever more."

MacArthur watches from home. A strange emotion takes hold of him. He is prepared to cringe in humiliation as soon as she opens her mouth. Instead, he's impressed. She isn't acting like a lunatic. Plus the firemen nod their heads in solemn agreement every time she makes a point. It looks like a press conference.

The night grows colder and colder and a sharp wind whips across the platform. Our Lady's halo grows dimmer and dimmer and disappears with a pop. Only then does Lili Marlene (Hadewig) turn to Ervin and tell him she's ready. Even then she hardly feels the cold, hardly feels at all her own foolishness as she stumbles over the rungs of the ladder in Mom's galoshes and Ervin saves her with a mighty hand.

Ervin takes her aside. The possibility of a psych evaluation has been discussed. They'd need to impound her car.

"Would I have to go someplace overnight? My brother can't take care of himself. He doesn't have anybody else," she says.

"Sorry, we forgot about that. I haven't seen your brother in years. Go explain this to the chief, he might let you off."

She stands next to the chief's vehicle just as he's calling the psych ward to get her a bed.

She lowers her eyes, a mute apology for having a laugh at his expense. The chief has had countless laughs at her expense over the years, but at this point, what does it matter? She needs to get home. The chief states his terms. She listens humbly, agrees to everything.

Ervin drives Lili Marlene (Hadewig) home in her own car.

"Hadewig. It's my new name," she says to Ervin.

"How so?" he says cautiously.

She remembers him as a gentle boy with a simple faith.

"I saw Our Lady up there. She gave me a new name."

He whistles softy. "Gosh. Ms. Chizek, that's really something. A miracle. But I'd be real cautious about who you tell this to. A lot of people will take it the wrong way. The chief, for example."

"Hadewig isn't a pretty name. Not like Lili Marlene," she says.

"It suits you better."

"I guess I'll get used to it."

The wind howls. The Vest's Christmas lights are dancing crazily as Ervin pulls the Crown Vic into the garage.

MacArthur sits in his chair in the garage doorway. He nods to Ervin. He looks at Lili Marlene in a way he hasn't in a while.

"I have a new name. Hadewig."

He opens his mouth but no words come out.

He follows her into the kitchen. She sits at the table and closes her eyes for a few seconds. She smiles to herself.

She takes out a mixing bowl.

"I saw my old classmate, the guy who works the fish counter at ValuRite. What's his name," she says, diverting him from whatever he's getting ready to confront her with.

"Boob Gryffyd," he says.

"Oh, yeah. How could I forget?" Usually he retreats to his bedroom and the internet while she makes dinner.

"Margaret called," he says. "She and the kids can't make it tomorrow because of the blizzard. They saw you on the news." Margaret is their cousin.

"Too bad they're not coming," she says.

"So we won't be having a Christmas party this year. We'll have to watch 'Mr. Magoo's Christmas Carol' all by ourselves." He's fallen into his habitual moroseness. He's expecting her to reminisce, the way she always does this time of year, about Mom and Pop, and how they're in the cold, cold ground, and how they loved Christmas.

"The kids don't care about 'Mr. Magoo's Christmas Carol,'" she says, flaring up. "They have their own shows and I'm afraid we'll never understand what they like and what they don't."

"What happened out there?" he says, feeling his way. He's usually the only one allowed to be testy.

She pauses, shrugs. "Sorry, MacArthur. A miracle happened to me."

"You're lucky," he says.

"Maybe," she says. "You're good looking and smart. I'm not."

"But on the other hand, neither of us has ever got married or had a kid," he says.

"We're the end of our line," she says.

"Maybe a good thing," he says.

"I don't know. Why did you never get married?" she says.

"I always had more important things to do." He doesn't ask why she never got married.

"Our parents had something special," she says. "But they didn't make a big deal of it."

"Well, maybe, but they picked names that scarred us for life. Hadewig isn't much better. Are you going to be able to live with that?"

She shrugs. "I will."

He opens the gallon jug of Old Sporran and fills a Christmas mug. Lili Marlene rolls out a pie crust, cuts four slits into it, arranges it over the pie plate. She works the heads of four fresh sardines out of the slits so their big round eyes are looking straight up, pointing in all four directions.

"What's that?" he says.

"Star gazy pie," she says. "To celebrate the birth of the Christ Child. See, they're looking straight up to heaven, where Mom and Pop and Baby Jesus and Our Lady are looking down at us." She brushes egg yolk over the crust.

"Did you plan this before you had the... vision?"

"No. I got the idea later, from talking to somebody."

"Did you have some kind of premonition? I'm curious about how it works."

"Yes. Not that I knew *exactly* what was going to happen," she says, looking at him uncertainly.

He could never tell how real her naïveté was. That was an attribute of medieval saints, he read someplace. Naïveté, uncertainty about themselves, certainty only about their faith.

"Pour me a mug," she says.

He looks up from his own mug. "Really?"

"Yes," she says.

"Cheers." They clink mugs.

She sips, gags, swallows.

The scotch burns all the way down.

In a few seconds, the light in the kitchen melts into gold. Her pupils dilate. Mom's cat clock rolls its eyes, swings its tail, overwhelming her with affection.

Sagging with laughter, she slams her mug on the pearly tabletop. "Jonathan Winters! On Jack Paar! Remember the time he pretended the stagehand crawling around on the scaffolding was his grandmother?"

MacArthur watches her with hooded eyes. He nods his head and cackles.

"You look like a turtle," she says.

He freezes, bares his teeth in a chilly smile.

He's holding three sky blue juggling balls. They're lit from within, little earths seen from the moon. He juggles them for a few minutes, then loses his rhythm and they drop and bounce, scattering across the floor, sending Fluffy streaking into the living room.

"Wow!" she says.

He sips from his mug, pleased.

She puts an LP on the stereo console. The music, a Christmas organ medley, thunders forth. They don't make Christmas albums the way they used to, they agree.

The aromas of baking pie crust, browning butter, simmering onions and fresh fish fill the room. She hangs a wreath on the inside of the door singing, *Lully, lullay, thou little tiny child.*

"Whoa, sister!" MacArthur says, choking, wide-eyed.

In the doorway Our Lady is smiling and nodding to the music. The Baby Jesus in her arms is jumping for joy.

Hadewig gasps, "MacArthur!"

He juggles the balls. The baby claps and laughs.

"Anselmus," Our Lady says. "It's your new name."

"Um, okay," he says.

Fortune Cookie Crumbles

William Harry Harding

She gets the worst fortunes—
          Land is always on the mind of a flying bird—
whether she chooses the cellophane-wrapped little cookie
from the two sitting on the plate or I hand one to her.
I get the best fortunes:
          You will inherit a large sum
          of money from an unusual source.

Neither of us puts any faith in these fortunes
but their imbalance has taught us to avoid
Chinese restaurants on special occasions,
like anniversaries. Especially anniversaries.
 2010—Hers: *It doesn't matter. Who is without a flaw?*
          Mine: *You will get what your heart desires.*

She refuses to swap hers for mine, accepting martyrdom.
She even joked about what we got last Thursday:
"Mine said, *A feeling is an idea with roots,*" she told our daughter.
"His was, *Soon you will be sitting on top of the world.*"
A worrier like her mother, our daughter didn't laugh.
Near tears, she hugged me: "It could mean heaven."

I put my arms around both of them, holding on:
          Never cut what you can untie.

Certain Questions

Regina Morin

I never should have married you,
You, with those worn, brown slippers
with their sad lips of matted fur.

I never should have been so
ga-ga over your bright brown eyes,
your willing mouth.

Was I so damned crazy in love that
could overlook those plaid shirts
and baggy pants that moaned
in the rear of your bachelor's
closet? How could
I love the poster of the matador,
his painted yellow thighs a
minor hoot of masculinity?

How could I, for fifty-four years
keep my willingness to be

a mistress of diminishing
hormones so intact that
I rise each morning to make
your coffee and pour it
into your favorite ceramic cup,
certain that worn brown slippers

and ancient matadors are
worth their weight in gold?

The Dance of
The Paper Lanterns

Dare DeLano

CHAPTER 1
Victoria Peak, Hong Kong, 1899

I have not always been Chinese.

Though the wizened old women who work the rice fields laugh when I tell them this. Gau Su strikes a gnarled hand on her thigh, whistles through her remaining teeth, and clasps me warmly on the shoulder. But Lao Ping narrows her eyes, loudly spits out the phlegm that troubles her throat, and says nothing. To her, I will always be a *gwai-lo*, a foreigner.

Despite their grudging allowance, I am at home here, where the sun streaks gold across the craggy hills, and the earth is just moist enough to make soft kisses below my feet when I walk. I settle the long green stalks in my basket and continue along the neat rows, bending and adding to the pile for as long as my weak back will let me. They wonder why I come, why I slog through wet fields and labor like a peasant, rather than sit in the big house, sipping tea and receiving callers. I do not wonder at it. At my age, it does not matter what others think, and I have no one left to curb my eccentricities. I am here because it is my home.

It is when I return up the hill, to the stone house with large rooms and cold floors that I feel out of place. Once inside, the houseboy Chan stokes the fire to warm my old limbs, and I shed my muddy cloak and boots. A warm woolen blanket lies over the arm of my easy chair. I sit and reach for the silver letterbox beside me. I lift the top of the box and carefully remove a large stack of letters. Below them is a worn leather-bound diary; I trace my hand along its face, along the initials long ago gilded: *CMH*. This has been my joy of late, to remember. I gently slip off the velvet ribbon that holds the letters together. Chan brings my tea, seasoned with honey. I sip slowly and close my eyes.

I pull the quilt up over my lap and rock back in the chair. The warmth of the fire does not reach my limbs as it used to. I know somehow that my life in this world is coming to a close. I no longer look forward to the Holy days, to the change in seasons, or to the lash of the monsoon striking out in God's glory. I look instead at where I began. I look instead to those moments in my life before I made the choices that would alter everything. Would I have done differently if I had known what would transpire? I do not know. I only know now that there are some secrets that bind us together, and some secrets that tear us apart. And that sometimes, the same secret will do both.

I close my eyes, and once again I am on the open sea with my life before me.

CHAPTER 2
South China Sea, 1851

The first time I saw Ming Li, she sat high above me on a gilded litter with brocade curtains, her shiny black hair set atop her head with ivory combs. Our ship was docked at Macao, a mere day's journey from our final destination of Hong Kong. I stood with Father beside the rail, his knuckles white as he held my letter to Edward. I stayed silent and watched as Ming Li rose up from the ramp born by her servants, impossible and lovely, like Aphrodite rising from the sea.

I stared as the bearers held her sedan chair steady against the small rocking of the ship, as if it were nothing. But Father seemed not to notice. He stood beside me at the rail, his jaw clenched.

"Did you know there would be Chinese coming on board Father?" I asked.

Father simply shook his head dismissively. "A merchant and his daughter. It is no concern of yours."

"But a woman?" I was incredulous. "Mrs. Clarkson says the Chinese women stay at home and that we should never expect to see a woman of rank in public."

"Do not change the subject," Father's voice was stern.

I turned from the spectacle and watched instead the frothy white-caps of the waves, their soft break, break, break against the ship reminding me of Tennyson. Father slowly loosened his grip on the paper, letting the wind take it. It floated softly down, twirling before it touched the surface of the water. I saw my words; clear for only a moment before bleeding onto the paper. Then it was gone.

Father cleared his throat. "No more letters," he said. "It is time to put an end to this and move on."

We stood in stubborn silence as a gull rose from its perch on the mast behind us and gently flapped toward shore.

"Do you imagine that I could do that so simply?" I kept my voice steady. "You may think otherwise, but this ocean means nothing. Not even this vast expanse of space could create a true distance between Edward and me."

Father sighed heavily. "You are young, and it is in your nature to be overly dramatic, but really, darling, this is too much." He raised his eyebrows and shook his head. "Mr. Chapin has not a penny to his name. The idea is preposterous." Father's chest filled with air as he spoke; his sturdy frame seemed to expand as well.

My hands gripped the rail tightly, but I took care to hold my anger inward. "I have given no thought to his income," I replied. "It is not a factor I care about in the slightest."

Father opened his mouth, then closed it again. He pursed his lips and shook his head. "Perhaps not. But I wager it is a topic he has considered in great detail." He seemed to soften then, becoming aware of frenzy of activity surrounding us. Beside us, one of the crew lunged about, fighting with a rope from the mast line.

"Are your trunks ready below?" he asked.

I nodded. Although we would not reach our destination today, and possibly not even the next, Mother and Nelly and I had our things packed and ready. Father turned away and walked toward the captain who had begun readying the ship to pull out of port.

The ship swayed sharply and I gripped the rail. The salt sting of the air sat heavy in my throat, and I swallowed. It was no matter. Whatever Father said, I knew that Edward would come for me.

I turned again toward the ornate sedan chair, the bearers standing on the rocking deck as if it were nothing. The young woman drew back a corner of the curtain and gazed out upon the deck. Her face was powdered white, her cheeks red. Her silken tunic of blue and gold shone in the early afternoon sun. She looked perhaps of a similar age to me. When she glanced my way, our eyes met and her gaze held me fast. I was certain I saw the traces of a smile before she pulled the heavy brocade curtain down and closed off her view. It was not long before she was borne down below deck, and although I looked for her often the rest of the day, I did not see her.

CHAPTER 3

Dearest Edward,

The swell of the sea troubles my sleep. Once awake I can think of nothing but you. And now that I sit down to write, by the precious light of the oil lamp, the rocking of the ship once again vexes me, making my hand so unsteady I fear you will not be able to read this letter. Indeed, it may not even find its way to you, for we have already passed three sacks floating on the sea which, after the men pulled them aboard, they found filled with letters bound for Macao. The crew showed no surprise, it being not uncommon for the natives to give up their task and cargo once they reach the open sea. But if I have one chance in one thousand to reach you, then I will write one thousand letters.

We have been ninety days at sea thus far, and although our destination is now in sight, it seems it will never end. Father is still cross with me. I do my best to pretend. But I shall never forgive him for forcing me away from you. He does not believe me when I tell him that neither the roiling ocean, nor the empty years ahead, nor even the strange land I am consigned to could ever come between us. When I speak so he all but forbids me to read Byron ever again, for he insists I am being overly romantic. And if he knew of our promise to each other, I shudder to think of his reaction.

So I have kept our secret safe. It is only Nelly whom I trust to see my tears, which I save up during the day when watchful eyes are upon me, and let flow only in the solitude of a sunset on deck or a stolen moment in our cabin while Mother and Father sup. For truth be told, solitude is rare, and I am most often in the company of a motley mix of crew and other passengers.

When you are able to write, you must send me a poem. I have the last you wrote clutched to my heart always. But I wish one written for me. If I can hold in my hand a reminder that you will come for me, perhaps this longing, which I feel so deep to my core that it is sometimes impossible to draw breath, will become tolerable. I will wait for it, as I will wait for you,

Forever,

Catherine

I read my letter through once. It was too full of yearning and self-pity, yet I folded it carefully and set the seal. I lay in the darkness listening to Mother's troubled tossing, Father's steady breaths. But between the rocking of the vessel and thoughts of Edward, sleep would not come.

Finally I could bear the cramped quarters no longer. I placed my feet on the warped floorboards, slipped on my overcoat, and opened the creaky cabin door with care. Once in the narrow hallway, I was already defying Father. He had instructed the first day on the ship that I should not wander by myself. Yet I felt invisible—and defiant. That his inheritance of a business concern halfway round the world should take us so far away from everything I had known in my seventeen years seemed an unfairness so great, I would never recover. And I would not yield quietly.

I found my way silently up to the deck. Standing by the railing, the wind full on my face, I felt the exhilaration of the unknown. The black sea swirled below me, cavernous and eternally deep. The night sky was bright with the moon and alight with stars. I wondered if Edward stood on his balcony in London looking up at the same sky. I pictured his brown hair falling into his eyes, and the way he flipped his head just a little whenever it did so. I saw him again as he left Father's study, his head bowed, shoulders bent. And how he shook his head just slightly as he met my eyes.

Heavy footfalls behind me interrupted my reverie. I turned swiftly and saw one of the sailors, swaying toward me.

"Evenin' Miss," he said, his words slightly slurred.

I turned quickly back around to look out at the water. He would never have dared speak to me if it were daylight.

"Oh," his voice was loud with drink. "To good to speak to me, then, are ya?"

Before I could even turn around, I felt his rough hands gripping my shoulders, his body pressing against my back. There was a deep cackle of laughter as the man held me tightly to him. From his arm came a rank, dirty smell, and there was foul breath, heavy with whisky as he spoke.

"T'aint no place for a lady, out at night with not a soul to protect her." His words were laughing and rough. The one hand held me tight against the rail, my arms pinned, and the other hand traveled, pulling up my nightclothes. I was so stunned it did not occur to me to scream. I had no idea what to do in my panic—it seemed difficult for me even to breath. I was frozen in fear. Father had warned me. Mother had warned me. I had laughed off their warnings of the rough sailors without a care in the world, as if I were somehow untouchable.

I struggled against him as he lifted my nightdress to my waist—
suddenly I remembered my voice and cried out. But his reaction
was quick, and he clasped a hand over my mouth almost before any
sound had escaped. He groaned deeply and struggled to pull down
his trousers. I strained against him, felt the ache in my chest where
I was pushed up against the ship's rail. I could barely breathe.

Suddenly there was a sickening sort of "thunk," and the man
went limp and fell against me. His arm around me slackened and
I pulled myself sharply around as he slumped to the deck. There
stood the slim Chinese girl I had watched earlier that day, her hair
long and loose, her face free of the white makeup. Her eyes were
wide, and in her hands she held a thick, iron bar. She stared at me
and I at her, my breath still coming fast.

"Thank you," I said finally, my voice sounding small and broken
in the night. And at the absurdity and smallness of my words under
the circumstances, I caught a small sob in my throat.

"You are hurt?" She asked, her words clipped and halting.

Even in my shocked state of mind I wondered at her ability to
speak English. I shook my head. "No," I whispered, for my voice
would not come completely. My hands shook as I straightened my
underthings and pulled my cloak around me. I sank to my knees,
then sat heavily, my legs unable to stand. The girl sat beside me,
holding the iron bar out in front of her as if she did not know what
to do with it. The man lay in front of us on the deck. We watched
him in silence; his body splayed unnaturally, his face turned towards
us so that we could see the brown teeth in his open mouth, and so
that we could not escape the fact that his eyes remained open,
unseeing.

The sea rose up suddenly and the girl beside me turned, leaned
over the side of the ship underneath the railing, and retched.
I realized then why she had been on deck at this time of night. I
understood her discomfort, for in the first leg of our voyage I had
done the same.

My mind was racing with the implications of the body that
lay before us. For there was no doubt in my mind by now that it

was merely a body, no longer a man. When the ship awoke at first light, we would have to explain. No one would question that the sailor had laid his hands on me—that was believable enough. But there would be many sailors who would be angry at the death of their brother at sea. Those at least would want to believe that he had succeeded in violating me, and I could easily imagine that the story would spread. It would only be a rumor, one that my father would work to squelch as quickly as possible. But rumor had ruined women with higher position than me. Even if I could go on despite it, would Mother ever survive the taint it would bring on our household? The merest question surrounding my virtue would devastate her.

The young woman beside me wiped her mouth with her sleeve and again sat beside me. I glanced at her, and saw the fear in her eyes, the quickness of her breath. For the weapon in her hand posed an even greater threat to her. For even in my inexperience I knew that a British ship was ruled by British law, and that the Captain had absolute power. What would his reaction be to a native taking the life of one of his own? Would the girl hang for the simple act of saving my virtue, possibly my life?

Our eyes met. Neither of us knew what to do or say. I turned my head and watched the water below, that vast expanse of black ocean as far as the eye could see. Her gaze followed mine. We looked at each other and did not have to speak a word. I moved to grab the man's shoulders, she moved to grab his feet. We stayed on our knees, dragging the limp weight over so that his entire body lay lengthwise against the side of the ship. There was a space between the deck and the railing—without a word we pushed, and the body slipped silently over the side. The soft splash when it hit the water was barely audible. And by the time I gained the courage to peer out over the water, there was no trace of it. The girl tossed the metal bar into the water as well and it sank swiftly.

There are bonds between sisters, shared blood running through their veins, bonds that can never be broken. But I knew in that moment, another kind of bond just as strong; that of a secret that must never be shared.

We stayed on our corner of the deck in silence, our hands clasped together without even realizing it, until the merest tinge of pink light became visible on the horizon. When we finally rose to go, I did not want to leave her. She seemed an oasis of safety, and I kept hold of her hand in mine.

Suddenly, there was a shape at the entrance of the companionway. I froze in fear. But the girl beside me spoke in a sharp tone in her native tongue. A male voice came from the doorway, hushed strange words. They bantered back and forth—it must have been only a short while but it felt like forever, while I stood helpless, waiting.

Finally the girl turned to me. "It is my brother," she said simply. She dropped my hand, with no further explanation, and walked away, her steps lovely and lilting as though she floated across the heavy wooden planks. Before I could recover my voice to ask if he had seen, if he knew, they were gone.

Only after I was back in my cabin, curled in a ball on my bed, and shaking although it was not cold, did I realize I did not even know her name.

Holding The Line: An American Family in Saigon

Marty Eberhardt

CHAPTER 1
Arrival
Chicago, January 1962

M y husband brought home such enticing pictures of Saigon. Chris held up color photos of huge trees shading French colonial architecture, sidewalk café menus handwritten on chalkboards, beautiful young girls bicycling by, their long silk tunics flying like kites behind them. White-haired old men sold fruits so strangely beautiful that I wanted to pluck them out of the picture and have a taste. My thoughts ran to soft tropical evenings, gourmet French meals, the adventure of a new culture, no snow shovels, and arresting the spread of communism, to boot. I figured I'd be a fool to quash Chris's sudden eagerness to join the diplomatic corps. It didn't hurt that I'd be trading in my role as Brownie troop co-leader for the job of representing my country in a foreign land. The weather in Chicago that night was equally convincing; I looked out the window and watched my neighbor's car spew brown muck all over the snow in front of our house. I turned up the thermostat and made up my mind to support Chris's wild idea.

Our four-year-old son Luke was equally enthusiastic.

"Nobody in my class has ever been on a jet plane!" said Luke, bouncing on the sofa cushions, his blonde curls flying. So Chris had two votes for his plan to convert from a journalist to a diplomat. The only holdout was our nine-year-old daughter, Ellie, who had the wrinkled-brow look she'd been cultivating lately.

"Daddy, did you say there's a war there?"

"Yes, honey, the North is fighting the South; the country's divided in half, like in Korea. The communists, called Viet Cong— the VC— are fighting the democracy in the south, where we'll be living. But you don't need to worry. The fighting's far away from Saigon." Chris and I talked a little more after the children went to bed, but it was settled quickly. We left in four months.

Saigon, May 1962

The flight from San Francisco to Saigon took twenty-eight hours, and I didn't remember sleeping through any of it. When the doors of the jet opened, I felt a blast of heat familiar to me only from an oven on broil. I took a deep breath of that lung-scorching heat, squeezed my little boy's hand, and followed my husband out the door. His blue seersucker suit had hardly a crease as he raced down the plane's steps with those long strides; his polio leg didn't hold him back a bit. My new linen traveling dress was already sticking to my skin with sudden sweat, and I felt anything but energetic. Chris pulled Ellie along with him. Her straw hat hung at an odd angle on her neck, and her sailor dress was stained with airplane pudding. She had a fierce frown and those skinny white legs were barely keeping pace with her father.

On the tarmac, we found ourselves surrounded by seven or eight Americans. There was also a young Vietnamese man with "WELCOME CHRIS AND SALLY VOGEL!" printed with red Magic Marker on a piece of typing paper. Was the tarmac melting under my feet? We shook hands through a sort of reception line, and the Vietnamese fellow, who seemed to be named Trang, snapped lots of Polaroid pictures. He gave Luke a photo, which the little boy held reverently against his chest. A big, bald, pink-faced man presented Chris with two large bottles filled with distilled water. Oddly, they were gin bottles.

***

Trang helped us through customs, and then the bald man, Bob Someone, bundled us into a taxi and said he'd follow. We were to go to our new home, recently vacated by Chris's predecessor, Bill Hardy, at the United States Information Service, or U.S.I.S.

Ellie stared at the holes in the taxi floor, which revealed a street full of enormous potholes and occasional rotten fruit. I looked out the window, feeling increasingly dizzy as our cab wove between bicycles, bicycle-driven chairs, motorcycle-driven chairs, small children darting about with no visible parents, elderly people crossing the street with huge baskets of food, seemingly unfazed by the erratic traffic, and a few cars, as well. The traffic didn't seem to travel in actual *lanes*. The smell of diesel mingled with the unmistakable scent of urine.

We passed some sort of patrol on a side street. Soldiers with guns had stopped a car. There was barbed wire behind them. I hadn't seen pictures like this when Chris gave us his photo tour. I should have paid more attention to that contradiction, but there was no time to discuss it, as my attention was diverted to a cacophony of quacking. A limousine with darkened windows had sped by and nearly upset a bicycle with two baskets full of ducks.

"Ducks! Ducks!" cried Luke, who was the only one simply enjoying the strangeness. He bounced on the taxi seat, just as he'd done on our couch in Chicago. I remember thinking that at least some things remained the same.

Our cab and Bob's car stopped at a gate. The stone wall next to it was topped with three feet of barbed wire. Apparently, this was the gate to our new house. I was about to ask Chris why we needed all that protection when Bob honked, and a stooped, elderly Vietnamese man in a white shirt, black pants, and plastic sandals unlocked and opened the gate, nodding his head as we entered. We piled out of the cars in front of a two-story stucco house that was decorated with an eight-foot-long concrete yellow lightning bolt under green and pink clouds. Once again there was a greeting party, composed this time of the old man and two Vietnamese women.

"Who are they?" I asked Bob.

"The servants."

"You mean they come with the house?"

"I expect they hope to. You can fire them if need be," he responded with a shrug.

My dress now clung to me, from shoulder to knee, with more sweat than I'd ever generated playing tennis. Sticky hairspray glued my hair to my cheek and neck, and I looked at Chris's blonde crew cut with envy. Bob was explaining to Chris that the street was named after South Vietnamese President Ngo Dinh Diem's older brother, Ngo Dinh Khoi, who'd been killed by the Viet Cong. I noticed that one of the women had black lacquer on her teeth. All of them. I did a double take when she broke into a smile and did a little bow toward me. According to Bob, the lacquer was supposed to be beautiful, and might also prevent tooth decay. Ellie transferred her concern from the holes in the taxi floor to the black teeth.

"Daddy, how can she chew with that black stuff on her teeth?"

"I don't know, sweetie. Maybe one of us can learn enough Vietnamese to ask her."

The old man started to speak French. We knew that this was the language we'd need to use here; the country had been a French colony from the late 1800s until eight years ago. Well, the Japanese took over for a while during the Second World War, but then the French returned for a few more years. So the Foreign Service said that we'd need French, because Vietnamese was awfully hard for westerners to learn. But I was having trouble with the accent.

I understood that the old man's name was Hien and that he'd worked as a cook for four Frenchmen and Mr. Hardy, who had preceded us in this house, as well as in Chris's job. Hien had learned how to cook in a French restaurant, he said. We seemed to be involved in some sort of a job interview, but I was hardly going to send Hien away. What would I do then? I nodded at Hien, and said, in my college French, that I would be delighted to work with him.

He was maybe five-foot two, and wiry. He had an old man's stoop. My mother would have called him a "tough old bird." I thought he was about seventy, but I knew, even then, that I couldn't age him using my usual criteria. Hien explained that the younger of the two women— the one with the black teeth— was his wife. She did laundry and *"beaucoup de choses"* (lots of things). Hien nodded his head and wrinkled his brow as he said this, and it was clear the two of them came as a package. I told him that was *"bon,"* and his face relaxed.

Hien's wife was named Thi Sau. I asked Bob how to spell it. Thi Sau had few lines in her face; I guessed she was about thirty-five— about half Hien's age. Bob said she probably came from further north. The black teeth were his clue. Chris had told me there were lots of refugees from the communist north, and I wondered briefly about her story. Thi Sau didn't speak any French, so I'd have to go through Hien to talk to her. Thi Sau studied the floor during the entire discussion.

Hien introduced Thi Ba as his sister. She looked closer to his age. There were deep, deep lines on her forehead. She was tiny— maybe about eighty-five pounds—but she looked strong and there was something about her that reminded me of my Scottish great-grandmother, that good Christian woman who tolerated no whining. Hien said that Thi Ba was in charge of the house (except the *cuisine*, he noted, with a glance at his sister). Thi Ba spoke French with a loud metallic clang. Both women wore little buns, but a few strands had escaped from Thi Sau's. Thi Ba's was a tight, neat little gray knot. Both women were dressed in black silk pajama bottoms and white short-sleeved cotton shirts with snaps instead of buttons. They all wore plastic sandals. Their clothing looked about as comfortable as it could be, given the merciless heat.

Hien continued on after his introductions. Unfortunately, he said, there was no gardener, driver, or nursemaid for the little boy, but he could help me find these people. I almost quipped that three servants was plenty, but I kept silent and smiled. I was trying not to show what a rube I was. Probably most women in my position had already been on lots of posts. I, on the other hand, had been the wife of a journalist until quite recently, when Chris made this impetuous decision to join the Foreign Service. I'd lived in St. Paul, Poughkeepsie, San Francisco, and Chicago. Period.

Hien continued with some welcome news. He had made us some of his French vichyssoise soup. Would we like some?

"*Ah, oui, bien sûr,*" I replied gratefully. Hien sat us down at the rather worn dining room table that came with the house, and brought out some paper bowls with the best vichyssoise I'd ever tasted. It was *cold*, as Ellie said, and Hien got the balance of the chives and pepper and potatoes and cream just right. He did a half bow as he took the bowls away, and then Thi Ba came in and announced in her loud voice that she would take us up to our bedrooms. Downstairs, the only cooling was from huge ceiling fans that bore an uncanny resemblance to the ones in the bar in *Casablanca.* I nearly cried with relief when I discovered that the bedrooms had air conditioning. Nothing else registered through the jet lag, which seeped through my brain and every one of my limbs. I managed to tuck the kids in, peel off my wet dress, and sink into bed as Chris went on about how the concrete lightning and clouds on the front of the house were "Vietnamese modern" architecture, and did I notice that we were next door to a Buddhist temple? And then I was out. When I woke up, Chris had already left for the office.

Chris's Journal

5/21/62, 8 p.m. Ed Murrow is now head of this agency, and I trust him, a veteran newsman. He said, "Truth is the best propaganda and lies are the worst."

Lord knows I hope he's right. Because there's no doubt I'm in charge of creating propaganda.

How did I get here? Probably intoxication with Kennedy's "Ask not what your country can do for you." All these years of reporting and seeing the pain and injustice and horrors of the world. Maybe a chance to do something about them. Reports of the Viet Cong atrocities that came out during the short time that refugees were allowed to flow from North to South Vietnam in the fifties... those affected me. Nine hundred thousand people, mostly Catholics, fled the North. And then of course there was the French colonial era... the malaria, the malnutrition, the dysentery on French rubber plantations. Twentieth century slavery. Twelve thousand people dying on one plantation over twenty-five years or so.

If I am honest with myself, it may be that I am still seeking the sense of heightened reality, the true sense of mission, the comradeship that came from fighting in the Pacific theater almost twenty years ago. I was no watcher then, no reporter. Maybe I can make a difference here.

And then, I knew this post would appeal to Sally's sense of drama. I imagined her, tanned arms gesturing madly, sweeping aside those long blonde bangs to expose brown eyes glowing with the exoticism of it all. I saw her wrapped up in some story so much more diverting than those of the Chicago suburbs. She'd have tales to tell her Vassar pals. Even with a husband who was only a mid-level bureaucrat, she'd have servants, as she had as a child in Saint Paul. She'd be a natural for the diplomatic corps; she'd pull me out of my fundamental introversion, as she always does. Usually to my benefit. She could use those ten years of French class. And the children would learn French, as well. (I must say the language classes the State Department gave me didn't get me very far).

In short, in the best-case scenario, I'll be helping my country to make the world a better place, and providing an unforgettable adventure for my family.

I'm hopeful about that first thought. The second is inevitable.

The Students Who Never Came to Class

Sandra Yeaman

Until Romania's communist president, Nicolae Ceasescu, was ousted and executed in December 1989, one of the few ways for an American to work in that country was through an educational program such as the Fulbright-Hayes Educational Exchange. That program allowed me to teach English at Alexandru Ioan Cuza University, the oldest university in Romania, for the 1977-1978 academic year.

As the American lecturer, I was expected not only to serve as native speaker of English, but also to introduce aspects of the American educational system to the students. The vast differences between the Romanian and the American university systems challenged me every day to decide how much of the American system to introduce and what to ignore.

I don't know what caused me to look up from my desk. I was in the English-language library, a room in an outlying, communist-era utilitarian building where most of the rooms contained stored university supplies. In less than a week I would leave Iasi, the provincial capital in the northeast of Romania. When people in Iasi referred to *the university*, they meant the impressive nineteenth-century, five-story building on the main street that filled three or four blocks where all classrooms, department offices, and administration offices were located. I doubt most people even knew the university had other buildings.

Just outside the open door stood a young woman I had never seen before, holding a large bouquet of flowers. She entered the room and handed me the flowers.

"My name is Mariana Ionescu," she said. Her long, ebony hair rested in curls on her shoulders. Like nearly everyone in the country, she was thin. The country lacked sufficient food because government policy required exporting anything of value to accumulate hard currency.

"I am in the third-year French majors class. I am very sorry that I missed your classes. Can I talk to you about my grade?"

"Thank you, Mariana, for the flowers," I replied. "They are lovely, but I don't know what there is to talk about. I gave you a zero because you were never in class."

Mariana was one of seven French majors who hadn't attended a single one of my Tuesday and Thursday evening English conversation classes that semester. Earlier that week, when I was in the large room on the third floor of the main university building that served as the English Department, the only office for all the teachers, I opened the big blue book to record grades for my five classes.

The first stop each teacher made when entering the room was to check the blue book. Any teacher who answered the phone wrote messages in the book. A teacher wishing to meet with another teacher wrote instructions in the book. Class assignments, staff meetings, even information about the funeral of the husband of one of the teachers were written in the book. And that's also where, at the end of each semester, teachers recorded students' grades.

That was the first time I saw the entire list of names. I had thought there were only seven students in that class, not fourteen. No more than five had ever attended at the same time. Several times, no one showed up. I had naively assumed that attending classes was one value the two university systems shared. Discovering not all students agreed stunned me. Since class participation was the only criterion for grading them, I assigned them all zeros.

"I know," Mariana said. "And I'm very sorry. Please let me explain. I am married, and our daughter was born in December. My husband's also a student, and we live far from the university. When I get home from classes in the afternoon, I don't want to leave my baby again. I have to be away from her so many hours each day. That's why I never came to class."

I had learned very early in the year that a Thursday evening class posed challenges to the students. They spent thirty to thirty-six hours each week in classrooms, with homework on top of that. And because all teachers, except the foreign lecturers, were expected to attend the weekly Communist Party meetings Thursday afternoons, no classes were scheduled then. That meant a Thursday evening class required students to return to the university after a break of several hours.

"Do you have other classes in the evening? Do you attend those?"

"No, your class was my only evening class."

I continued asking her questions to see how comfortable she was speaking English, and to gauge her sincerity. After about ten minutes I ended the conversation. "Thank you for your explanation," I said. "I can see now that your English is quite good. Because you had the courage to come to talk with me, I will consider changing your grade."

By now, at the end of my time in Romania, my respect for the Romanian people, especially the students, had grown tremendously as I observed how they persevered in efforts to overcome the suffering the government imposed on them. I experienced the shortage of food along with everyone else, having lost twenty pounds myself. But my students told me of other privations, such as the lack of functioning outlets in their dorm rooms. The authorities had sealed them off to limit energy consumption. If the students wanted to listen to a radio, they had to unplug the only light bulb in the room four of them shared and insert an adapter that included a socket as well as a receptacle for screwing the light bulb back in. But if the university authorities caught them, they would confiscate both the adapters and whatever the students plugged into them.

Life for the teachers improved only slightly.

***

I had two advantages over them. First, my stipend as a lecturer was about ten times what my Romanian colleagues received each month. Second, I could leave at the end of the academic year.

Two months before the end of my stay, the university finally gave the British lecturer, Chris, and me a room dedicated as the English-language library. The few sparsely filled shelves wouldn't have impressed anyone back in the US. Nonetheless, I was delighted to have this private space. Until then, the books—all donations from the UK and US governments through exchange lecturers such as Chris and me—had been effectively locked up on three shelves in one corner of the university's English Department. Chris had been in Romania the year before me and explained that if we gave the books to the university's library, the students wouldn't be allowed to take them out.

University libraries were considered for reference, not circulation, at least not for students. The teachers could remove books from the library—an example of the slight improvement— and keep them for as long as they wished. Students could not.

Yet my Romanian colleagues often assigned readings from books that were only available in the university's library and expected the students to find time to sit for hours, sharing a single book. I even overheard a conversation in which one of my colleagues admitted to another that he had assigned his students the task of copying thirty pages of *Beowulf* as homework, work that could only be done in the library, not at home.

In contrast, Chris and I controlled the contents of the new library and made the books available to the students. We invited students to come Tuesday, Wednesday, and Thursday afternoons to read, talk with us, and even to check out the books. While one of us was in the room, we kept the door open.

***

The next day, another of the missing students appeared, this time outside the English Department. The door was kept shut to ensure quiet and privacy for the teachers between classes. The closed door discouraged students from meeting with teachers in the room. None dared come into the room simply to look at the books. This student, therefore, showed more confidence than most by knocking on the door and telling the teacher who answered that she wanted to see me.

Again, I had never seen the woman in the corridor. "Mrs. Wenner," she said.

"Yes?"

"My name is Irina Popescu." She kept her eyes lowered, avoiding mine, as she spoke. "I heard from Mariana that if I come to see you, you will change my grade." Irina was shorter than Mariana, with straight blond hair, typical of the Germans and Hungarians who had settled in Romania centuries earlier. Their lighter skin, hair, and eye color contrasted with that of the native Romanian population, most of whom might be mistaken for being from Mediterranean countries such as Italy and Spain. Maybe it was Irina's northern European appearance, like my own, that made me feel some sympathy for her.

"That's not quite right," I said. "Mariana came to see me, showing courage. She apologized for not attending my classes. She explained her reasons for not coming back to the university in the evening. Based on those factors, I told her that I would *think* about her request. I did *not* tell her I would change her grade. I told her I would consider it. So why didn't you attend my classes?"

"I am a French major, not an English major. I didn't think English conversation is important."

My sympathy began fading at that point. "I'm sorry that's what you thought then. What do you think now?"

"I just want a good grade."

My sympathy completely gone, I said, "Then you should have attended my class. Seven of your colleagues did."

"Aren't you going to change my grade?" Irina asked, now looking me straight in the eye.

"You haven't given me any reason to change your grade."

She turned on her heels and walked away without another word.

The following day, yet another of the missing students appeared. She waited for me in the corridor.

"Mrs. Wenner," she said as she approached me, "my name is Adriana Niculescu. I want you to change my grade." Adriana stood solidly facing me, arms crossed and eyes firmly fixed on mine.

I could barely believe my ears. Such insolence. A complete contrast to the attitude I experienced from students in my other classes that year. "Well, Adriana, why should I change your grade?" I asked, aware that I hadn't totally suppressed the laugh that gave away that I didn't expect a reasonable response.

"You have to change my grade," she said. "If you don't change my grade, I'll have to take the class again, and that means you'll have to stay here this summer to teach it."

Adriana shifted her weight, keeping her eyes locked on mine. I bit my tongue this time before speaking. "You are right about one thing," I said. "If I don't change your grade, you'll have to take the class again. But that doesn't mean I have to teach it. The university will have to provide another teacher for the class."

Adriana wasn't satisfied. She moved her hands to her hips and straightened up. "You *have* to change my grade," she said. "Zero isn't a grade."

"Well," I said, "then I think that's perfect. I gave you no grade because you attended no classes."

Adriana swiveled away from me and stomped down the corridor. She was the last of the students to approach me about grades.

In the end, I changed Mariana's grade, from zero to four, the highest non-passing grade on the one-to-ten scale. I didn't change the other grades, but I left a note in the big blue book to explain why I had given six students zero. I left Iasi the next day and Romania two weeks later. I never learned if someone changed the grades I assigned.

But now and then I wondered if the students had to retake the class, or if one of the Romanian teachers had to lead it. Most of all, I hoped the students faced no more serious consequences. Their lives were difficult enough already.

Home Palindrome

Carrie Danielson

My foot dangles in the stream,
spotted rocks, slimy with green algae,
toes numb— cold glacier water,
heat radiates from my granite boulder.
I lie back and watch the sky.

Pines sway— their incense swirls,
pollen drifts and scatters through shafts of sunlight,
a blue jay squawks and flutters, defends his pinecone.
I close my eyes and hear
the chatter of golden aspen leaves.

Time stops, I breathe and breathe again
I could be five or fifteen or fifty
on this mica-flecked, ancient rock.
Each cell dissolves and disappears into time.
deep in the Rockies, deep in my home.

Deep in the Rockies, deep in my home,
each cell dissolves and disappears into time.
On this mica-flecked, ancient rock,
I could be five or fifteen or fifty.
Time stops, I breathe and breathe again.

The chatter of golden aspen leaves,

I close my eyes and hear
a blue jay squawk and flutter, defend his pinecone,
pollen drifts and scatters through shafts of sunlight,
pines sway, their incense swirls.

I lie back and watch the sky,
heat radiates from my granite boulder,
toes numb— cold glacier water,
spotted rocks, slimy with green algae,
my foot dangles in the stream.

Sunday Breakfast

Krishna Jagannathan

Every Sunday morning as a young girl, I would wake up to the full-bodied vocalizations of classical Indian music and the enticing aroma of homemade coffee. Although we owned more modern acoustic equipment, from which my beloved rock tunes blared during the rest of the week, a reel-to-reel player occupied pride of place in our family room and was the main feature on Sunday mornings. My father would painstakingly thread the magnetic tape from the feed reel through the guides on the player and wind it manually onto the take up reel. I thought it was a cumbersome and unnecessary process to play music that was equally out of date, and I would constantly try to persuade him to give the player away because it was a dinosaur compared to my sophisticated "boom box," which even had a socket for headphones so he could listen to the music privately. He would patiently wait through the exposition of my adolescent logic and then go back to tending to the antiquated machine. With a huff of exasperation, I would head to the kitchen where the decoction for the coffee was brewing on the stove.

That too was a process, which my father would oversee with the same exacting precision. Not for him the quick fix of Folgers crystals. Each month he would buy the beans fresh from the store, grind them himself in a coffee grinder and store them in the refrigerator for Sunday breakfast. He would pour the powder into the cappuccino maker, add water and let it work its magic. The milk was measured and heated with a little sugar in a mug in the microwave and he would stand in front of the microwave door, watching until the liquid rose to almost the top of the mug. Even though the cappuccino machine had an attachment to froth the milk, my father would pour the milk back and forth between two stainless cups until he was satisfied that it was foamy enough to top the coffee. Every Sunday, I would try to wheedle him into giving me a cup with breakfast, but he would merely raise his eyebrows indulgently, tell me I was not old enough yet, and hand me a cup of cold milk.

I was always fed healthy meals, which usually included the bane of my existence: fruit. I drank fruit juice but could never manage to reconcile myself to consuming the actual source that it came from. The mango is the king of fruit in my culture and Indians are genetically hard-wired to enjoy eating them, but I seemed to have missed inheriting that gene. I could never understand the fascination for such a slippery stringy fruit and sought to avoid eating it when I could, opting instead for doughnuts, cookies, or chocolate cake, junk food which was more pleasing to my westernized palate. One of my father's weekend breakfast routines was to cut the mango. It had been selected from the weekly stock ripening in the garage and chilled in the refrigerator overnight so that it could be skinned and sliced, which my father did with the expertise of a sushi chef. My portion would be placed on my plate and I could not leave the table until it had been finished. I would frequently attempt to bargain with him, saying that I would finish the mango if he would let me have a cup of coffee or play my own songs on Sunday, ashamed of the strange, seemingly barbaric music emanating from the reel-to-reel player. It never worked though, and I endured the weekly trial of music and mangoes with resignation, if not forbearance.

Years later, after having moved around the country due to professional and personal obligations, I returned home to visit my parents. I parked my car at the curbside of my childhood home and as I walked towards the door, I could hear the strains of the same Indian songs from my childhood coming from inside the house.

I moved from the door to look through the windows that fronted the family room. I could still see the reel-to-reel player on the shelf, reels rotating stolidly through the music. I rang the bell and my mother opened the door. After giving her a hug, I asked "So where's Dad?"

"He's in the kitchen, making coffee," she answered. I walked through the foyer into the kitchen, where, sure enough, my father was bent over the coffee machine on the kitchen counter, brows furrowed in concentration. I turned towards the kitchen table, noting that it was set as usual for breakfast. Of course it was mango season, and I smiled at the familiar sight of mango slices on a plate at the center of the table. I didn't see my milk mug in the usual place where I used to sit so I walked to the refrigerator to get the milk and then went to one of the cabinets to find a mug to pour it into.

My father's voice stopped me. "No, *beti*, I'm making coffee for you." Then he handed me a mug filled with the frothy concoction that had bedeviled my youth.

I sat down at the table and took a sip of the hot, sweet beverage, inhaling the aroma with satisfaction. Still, I knew there was something else that needed to be done to complete the ritual. I took my fork, reached towards the plate with the mango sections on it and slid a few pieces onto my plate. Bracing myself resolutely, I speared a bite with my fork and deposited it in my mouth. My eyes flew wide open as its sweet taste and smooth texture hit my taste buds. I stared across the table at my father, finally understanding, and then settled back in my chair to finish the rest of my breakfast while the exotic melody of Carnatic music percolated around me.

Belmont Park

Brenda Sako

El Cajon's summer heat doesn't bother me, but it makes my dad miserable, which makes me miserable.

"This stupid air conditioner not helping, man!" he says. He's barefoot, in bright orange shorts and no shirt. He stands in front of the small AC unit that sits in the living room window.

With heavy eyelids, I remind him that constant complaining doesn't help the heat *either,* but I don't say *constant complaining.* Instead, I use words he can understand.

"But only 8:30 a.m. and already too damn hot, man!" he says. His accent is heavy and his words just mere impressions, like he's singing along to a song he doesn't quite know the lyrics to.

He sits in the old green corduroy recliner and picks up the remote. His mood instantly elevates when he discovers that Iraq is playing Mexico. He turns up the volume and reclines the chair far back, so that his feet are dangling in the air, above the rest of him.

I force myself up, fold my bedding, and put it back in the linen closet. I sit back down on the bare couch.

"Do you want coffee?" he asks.

"Sure."

He measures two teaspoons of instant coffee into a Styrofoam cup, then fills it with hot water from the dispenser.

"Only cream, right?"

"Yeah, thanks," I say.

He sits back down, lights a cigarette, changes the channel to CNN. For a moment, I try focusing on the words, but the messages taste bitter and blurry.

He flips back to the soccer game for a few minutes, then back to CNN.

"I don't understand how people actually consider this *news*," I blurt out, without really meaning to.

"You don't understand anything," he says without looking at me, then he points the remote at the television and changes the channel back to the soccer game.

"That network is poisonous," I say, under my breath.

"Lydia, you don't know what you're talking about," he says with calm blue authority.

"I know what I'm talking about," I say, but he's easily provoked in this heat and so am I, so I back off. I go into his bedroom to get dressed and when I come back out into the living room, he's still on CNN.

"Can we watch something else?" I ask.

We watch the last fifteen minutes of *The Price is Right*. A heavy-set, middle-aged woman, dressed in a bright pink track suit, competes for a Ford Fiesta.

"Did she win it?" I ask.

"Yeah, she won. Don't you see that fat ass jumping up and down? "

My dad is what most people would also consider a "fat ass," but I could never figure out if he's oblivious to this fact or if he thinks being fat gives him license to talk like that. I ignore his question by getting up and walking to the kitchen, which somehow compels him to repeat it. I open the fridge and focus on my breath for a moment. A big block of yellow cheese stares at me.

"Are you hungry?" my dad asks, exhaling cigarette smoke in my direction.

"Is that your *second* cigarette?"

"Yeah, I smoke more when it's hot. Do you want breakfast?" he asks.

"You said the same thing when it was cold."

"No I didn't."

"Yes, you did. Just the other day, you said *I smoke more when it's cold*. I remember."

"I don't remember. Are you hungry? I can make you omelet."

"I'm good with this. Thanks," I say holding up my coffee.

"Omelette with green pepper?" he suggests again, but this time, he has a green pepper in one hand and he's dangling it a few inches from my face, like he's dangling a carrot in front of a rabbit.

"I don't like green peppers," I say.

He picks up the remote and changes the channel back to CNN.

When I remind him of our beach plans, he disappears into his bedroom and when he comes back out, he's wearing a turquoise blue tank top with the image of a generic yellow cartoon duck. The duck is wearing Hawaiian-themed swimming trunks and a bubble that hangs above the duck's head reads "Life's a Beach" in big bouncy letters.

When we get to Belmont Park, he chooses to park his car in the small lot behind the roller coaster. He picks a really tight spot and when I tell him to be careful, he says, "Don't worry. I'm not you. I know how to drive."

My dad has lived in San Diego for almost forty years, but this is his first time visiting Belmont Park. Last week, it was his first time visiting Coronado Island and Balboa Park. The week before, we watched the seals in La Jolla and the week before that, we did a Mission Trails nature walk. All first times for him.

He likes to tell the story of his first few days in America. Having fled Iraq shortly after Saddam Hussein took office, he began his treacherous journey to America. It took him a little over a year, then one Saturday afternoon, he finally arrived at Los Angeles International Airport. His eldest cousin, Jamal, picked him up and drove him south to San Diego. It took them nearly four hours to get there because of the LA traffic. That was the day, according to my dad, he decided he would never live in LA.

The next morning, Jamal took him to Sunday mass and, on Monday morning, he started a job at Green Field Market, a small market in a poor part of San Diego.

On average, he worked ninety hours a week and was given every other Sunday off. After several years of hard work, he bought his own market, but kept the same rigorous work schedule for thirty-eight years. Even with the birth of his three children, he never thought of reducing his work hours. Even after Jamal's youngest son was held up and murdered while working the register one night at Green Field Market, he never considered other options.

His knees hurt more than usual, so we walk at a snail-like pace toward Pacific Beach. I point ahead and tell him we should walk all the way to the pier and back. He laughs.

"Don't laugh. You can do it," I say.

"I'm too tired to walk on dialysis days," he says.

"I know, but we still have the other days," I gently remind him.

To go through what he was going through was unimaginable to me. Every Monday, Wednesday, and Friday, he had a five-hour date with a dialysis machine at a nearby dialysis center. Because his kidneys have stopped functioning properly, he has to depend on a machine to purify all the blood in his body. The process is taxing, taking him nearly eight hours of recovery time afterwards. In addition to kidney failure, he dealt with gout, diabetes, and arthritis. This has been his life for two years now and would be his life until a kidney transplant could be performed.

We sit on the wall that divides the boardwalk from the sandy beach. I sit facing the ocean. He sits facing the opposite direction. He people watches, focusing on attractive women in skimpy swim suits. The beautiful chaos serves as a powerful distraction from the heat. He seems to be in high spirits, making jovial and sometimes inappropriate comments, but mostly, the remarks are non-sensical. Luckily, the sounds of the crashing waves wash his words and all of language into an irrelevant abyss.

"Ready to walk again?"

"Let's go," he says.

"We can take another break soon, if you need one."

"I don't need a break," he says.

"Are you hungry?"

"Not yet."

He gives me a tour of the Museum of Obviousness.

"These are tourists," he explains as we walk. He points at a large group of young people wearing bright matching shirts and speaking in Italian.

"Dad, don't point at people like that. It's rude."

"So what? I'm not saying anything bad about them."

"I know that, but they don't know that," I say.

***

"You're too much," he says. Even though my mom and dad have been divorced for more than ten years, *You're too much* was something they both still said to me. It's a phrase translated very literally from Arabic. It meant I was too worried, too sensitive, too reactive, too concerned, just *too much*.

He continues the tour.

"The lifeguard is watching people swim," he says.

"Yeah, he is."

"He has to make sure nobody is drowning," he says.

"Yup, that's his job."

"The vacation rentals come with parking spots," he says.

"That's what it looks like."

"This car is from Arizona. Look at the plates," he says.

We take another break. This time, he sits right next to me and faces the ocean too.

A very dark and shiny young black man in colorful swimming shorts walks toward us and throws a soda can into the recycling bin near us.

"How long have we been walking?" my dad asks.

"Almost an hour."

"I haven't seen any black people."

"I've seen a few," I say.

"A few, but not too many."

"Are you hungry yet?" I ask.

"I'm very hungry. Do you know why?" he asks.

I jump to my feet, then I help my dad to his feet, giving him my shoulder to use for safety.

"Do I know why you're hungry?" I repeat the question back to him.

"I mean do you know why there aren't any black people here?"

"Um, no, not really. I don't think there's really like a reason."

"Because they're afraid of swimming."

"That doesn't sound accurate," I say and begin walking a bit ahead of him. I tend to walk ahead when I don't know how to respond.

"I'm getting very hungry now," he says.

"Okay, don't worry, we'll eat soon."

Two women eating vanilla ice cream cones walk past us.

"It's no good for my blood sugar go down."

"Okay," I say. "We'll pick a spot really soon," I assure him.

"I have to sit," he says.

"Are you okay?"

"I don't have much time," he says. He points at the dividing wall behind tower sixteen and tells me he's going to sit on the stairs beneath the tower.

"Okay! Stay there! I'll go get you an ice cream cone! I'll be right back!"

I run down the boardwalk, leaving my dad behind, my heart pounding under my skin, under the vicious sun.

The wait for ice cream is as long as the wait to ride Space Mountain. *Shit! He doesn't have much time left!*

I run back toward him, but even from a distance, he looks weak. I spot a nearby cart selling fruit.

"Hey dad! I'm getting this apple!" I give him a thumbs up.

He gives me a thumbs down.

"You don't want this apple?" I yell, but he's pretty far from me and I can't quite hear what he's saying, so I put the apple down and run back toward him.

"Why don't you want the apple?"

"I just don't want it!" he says with a sudden energy. "I thought you were getting ice cream!"

"I was, but the line is way too long! There isn't enough time! Just eat an apple. Take a few bites, so your blood sugar won't drop any further, okay? I'm going to get you that apple."

"No."

"Why not?"

"I don't like green apples!"

"They have fruit bars too. Should I get a fruit bar?"

"I don't want it. Stop asking me."

"Okay, well, what should I do then?"

"I need *real* food," he says. He points to Cowgirl Bar and Grill straight ahead of us.

"But we'll have to be seated to place an order. Can you wait that long?"

"I think so."

"You *think* so?"

"Well, maybe," he says.

"Dad, this is a sit-down-and-order type of place," I repeat.

"You don't want to sit down and eat with me," he says and then takes off down the boardwalk at a quicker pace than he'd walked all day.

He doesn't deserve to be followed and reasoned with, but he doesn't deserve to go into diabetic shock under the blazing sun, so I follow him and reason with him.

"Let's go eat at that grill," I say.

"No, just forget it," he says.

"The food will take some time to prepare. It's not quick."

"Are you in hurry? You need to go somewhere?" he snaps.

"You said you didn't have much time left, so I'm trying to help you!"

"Yeah!" he yelled.

"What do you mean *yeah*?"

"That means I have *some* time left!"

"No! It means you don't have time left and it's an emergency!"

"You're too much!" he says. "If I don't have no time left, I say I have no time left!"

"I wish you would have found the *time* to fucking learn English so we can have one normal conversation!"

At this, he falls totally silent and says he's not hungry anymore. I immediately regret what I said, I regretted it even while I said it, but I gave up on him, in that moment. I didn't have the energy.

"I'm going to get the car. Wait here," I say holding my hand out.

He fishes the keys out of his right pocket, hands them to me, then sits down on a large, flat rock and lights a Marlboro Light.

On my walk back to the car, I stop at the Dipping Dots stand. I order one small vanilla.

The young girl serves me. Her badge reads "trainee." "That'll be $4.50," she says.

I walk back toward my dad helping myself to three spoonfuls along the way.

Unlike my mother, who makes me beg for a truce after we argue, my dad has already forgiven me for the hurtful words. His smile immediately grows wider when he sees me walking back with dessert.

"Is that an apple?" he asks, cracking up at his own joke, which isn't even a joke.

"It's vanilla," I respond in a stubborn, deadpan way.

"That's alright," he says, "I *like* vanilla."

"I know that Dad. That's why I got vanilla."

"Yeah, it's okay," he repeats. "That's alright, I like vanilla."

"Dad, when you say *that's alright...*," I start to explain, but stop.

I leave him there in a happy state, eating vanilla Dipping Dots and smoking Marlboro Lights. Once more, I head to the car. I take my time all the way, stopping for a chocolate Dipping Dots.

"That ice cream hit the spot," he says when I finally pick him up from the big, flat rock I left him on.

"You look much better," I say.

"I *feel* much better."

"Good."

"Where are we eating?" he asks.

"I don't know," I say, "but I'm up for anything."

"Um up fur onni ting too," he says.

I pick Arcade Fire on Pandora, plug it in, turn it up, and push all noise into the background fabric of our day at the beach. The beauty and power of the ocean washes away all things that don't matter, revealing what truly matters is only what remains, that which is forever unchanged. The air is cooler now and its friendly caress soothes and heals us as we ride.

The Merry-Go-Round

Anthony Jesse

I'm working another Saturday morning at the merry-go-round and there he is again, shoulders hunched, hands stuffed into the pockets of his brown leather jacket, shuffling back and forth between one foot and the other. He doesn't look like a pedophile. I mean he's got a full head of hair and all. And he doesn't have that look. You know what I'm talking about—the one that creeps you out. Mostly he just looks sad, as if he's seeing something there no one else does. I always wonder what it is.

The other mothers and fathers avoid him when they realize he's there alone without any kids. They stand protectively between him and their children. Can't say I blame them. They haven't watched him as long as I have.

I've told Jim about him a couple of times. He's told me to keep away from him. He says maybe he's a stalker. He says a girl like me needs to be careful.

Today he's looking over at me as if he's trying to muster up the courage to approach me. He can't be trying to pick up on me? I must be half his age. Maybe Jim's right and he's a creep after all.

There is a lull in the number of people around the merry-go-round. Then he steps over toward my direction. I almost panic when I realize he's actually going to come up to me.

"What is it now, two bucks for a ride?" he asks, not really looking me in the eye.

"Two-fifty for five minutes."

"I'd like one, please."

This is weird. I take his money. He goes and stands near the merry-go-round while it slows down, but now a noisy crowd of parents and their kids swoop in. I'm busy taking money, but I keep an eye on the guy to see what he does. He looks back over at me and the others a couple of times. He looks uncomfortable. Then he abruptly leaves before the others queue up. He turns his head toward me only briefly as he escapes but not before I notice that he's crying.

***

I get home from work and Jim is already preparing dinner for me. It looks elaborate. He likes to cook, and he's good at it. Today he's got all my favorites out—some linguini waiting for the pot and some clams soaking. I realize how hungry I am.

"Why don't you go shower. I'll be finished by the time you're done."

I'm tired, and I'm grateful he's taking care of dinner. I go off to wash up.

I'm done with my shower and dressed now. I go out into the dining area and he's got the food all laid out, complete with my favorite Riesling.

"So how was work?" he asks as I sit opposite of him.

"Same as always," I say. I don't tell him about the man coming over and talking to me.

Jim talks a little about his day, and apparently his mother is taking a trip to England next month. Then he gets this look on his face. I know this look. I always get uncomfortable when he has that look. He's going to get all mushy on me.

"You know we've been together a long time now," he says.

I'm already afraid of where he's going with this.

"You know, with the promotion and all, I'll be making good money. We could afford a better place, maybe a more *permanent* place..." he says, trailing off.

I try to remain neutral.

"I mean... what I'm saying is... I'd like to spend my life with you."

He brings out a ring.

"Alex. Will you marry me?"

I don't say anything. I'm not sure what to say, or I should say, I don't know *how* to say it. I love Jim. And he's a perfect catch. He's good looking and affectionate. At twenty-nine he already has a great career. Not only does he cook, but he irons his own shirts. I'd be crazy not to accept.

"Jim," I say after an awkward silence. "I love you, I really do. But I'm not sure if I'm ready for that yet."

It sounds lame and I know it. He looks away. I see his eyes are watering. I feel like shit.

"Will you at least consider it?"

"Yes," I say as gently as I can. "I just need a little more time."

"I understand," he says. But I know he doesn't.

***

A couple of weeks have passed and things between Jim and me are almost normal. After work I go home and get ready for a night out. We're going out with Jim's friend, Gregg, and Gregg's wife, Tasha. I like Gregg all right, but Tasha, not so much. We're going for Indian downtown in the Gaslamp and then maybe to the Whiskey Girl for some drinks.

Over tandoori, palak, and naan, the conversation turns, as it always does, to biotech. All three of them work in the industry. I'm the only merry-go-round attendant.

"So Alexis, how's the park been?" Tasha asks, sipping her Cabernet and changing the subject. "Anything exciting going on?"

I hate it when she calls me Alexis. Not even my mom calls me Alexis. And I can never tell whether she's trying to make fun of me or honestly include me in the conversation. Either way, it's clear she doesn't think much of my *profession*. I suppose that's natural, but I always wonder why she never asks about my writing.

"Not really. I like it that way. It gives me time to think," I say.

"Alex has been busy writing these days," says Jim, sounding as if he were apologizing for me.

"Oh? About what?" she asks.

"I'm thinking about writing about a mysterious man who keeps coming to the merry-go-round all by himself."

"You're not talking about that guy are you?" Jim asks.

"What guy is this?" asks Tasha.

"There's a creepy old man that's been loitering around the merry-go-round on the weekends. I keep telling her that he might be a stalker or a pedophile or something."

"He's not creepy. And he's not *that* old. I don't think he's dangerous or anything," I say surprising myself at how defensive I am about him. "There's just something about him I can't figure out is all."

Tasha looks over with a raised eyebrow at Jim. Gregg puts down his fork and gives Jim a quick look as well. Jim gets this pained look on his face. It hits me that Tasha and Gregg must know that Jim proposed to me and that I've refused.

***

It's Sunday morning and I have a hangover, but I get up and am on time for work anyway. My coworker, Sam, and I slide out the wooden doors and open up the booth. She's a cheerful one, Sam—just like the damn animals. I hate them for that. It seems no matter how many crazy kids ride them, they're always smiling. It must be nice to be that positive.

After having defended him last night I think that guy owes it to me to show up today, and he does, right during Sam's meal break. Today my curiosity gets the best of me and I walk toward him. He notices and freezes. I smile my nicest and try to disarm him, but he turns and walks back toward the museums. This guy's a skittish one.

***

It's Friday, and I'm out Christmas shopping. I'm trying to pick out a gift for Jim. I'm thinking no clothes this time. It's gotta be good and personal to soften the blow of turning down his proposal. So I'm in a Williams-Sonoma looking at really nice wine goblets, but I know that won't work. He probably wants to forget the last time he served me my favorite Riesling. I sigh and make another run through the mall. I'm up on the top floor and pass by a toy store. I'm stunned for a second because I see that guy in there.

He's staring at a stuffed giraffe. And he's got that same look— you know, the one he has at the merry-go-round. But what really gets me is the giraffe. My father gave me one just like that when I was ten. That was just before he died. I'm starting to remember things now—things I don't want to think about—like the funeral, and the first Christmas without him. Then the man sighs and makes a move to leave. I jump quickly into the entrance of the shop next door. I peek my head out and see he has left the toy shop and is heading off toward the parking lot. I decide to follow him. I have to know what this guy is about once and for all.

Luck is with me. He's parked in the same lot as I am, but it looks like a little farther out. I reach my car first, get in and wait. He takes off and I follow him, keeping two to three cars between us. He heads down the eight toward Point Loma. Then he gets off the freeway and exits onto Rosecrans. I keep behind him wondering what kind of crazy I am to do this. Who's the stalker now?

Soon he's making a left, then a right. It looks like he's headed for the elementary school there. He parks his car, but I have to drive past him because I don't want him to see me. I circle back around the block. When I pass through again, he's out of the car and standing in front of the schoolyard watching the kids play during their lunch break. I'm starting to wonder if this guy's a perv after all.

***

It's past midnight, and I'm in the living room sitting on the couch in the living room. I'm in my robe, which glows a pale blue in the light cast by the moonlight shining through the window. I hear Jim's light breathing coming in from the bedroom. I like the way he breathes when he sleeps. Sometimes, when I'm awake in bed late at night, I listen to him while I spy on him. I always like the way his thick and curly dark hair frames his roundish face. He looks like a little boy. But tonight I'm not thinking about Jim. I'm thinking about my father.

I have just had a dream about Daddy. I was ten-years-old and we were walking through the zoo. We floated in and out of the different exhibits in an impossible sequence. And the exhibits were floating clouds circling the merry-go-round at work for some reason—you know how dreams are. Then we were looking at the giraffes. I was excited and pointing at their long necks.

I remember when I was little and we really were at the zoo I was surprised at how the giraffes stayed in their pens even though there was no wall hemming them in. My dad told me that was because they were afraid to step over the small concrete moat. It made me sad because I thought that all they had to do was take that step and they'd be free. But they never did. Anyway, back to my dream. At that moment I turned around to look at my dad, but instead of my dad it was that man. That's when I woke up.

I'm a little freaked out. I haven't thought about Daddy in a very long time, and now I've been haunted by him all day. And it's all because of that weird guy and that giraffe. I ask the moon why I dreamed that Daddy turned into that guy just when I've made my mind up that that guy's a perv. The moon doesn't answer.

***

It's Saturday and I'm nearing the end of my shift. I'm pretty tired on account of not getting enough sleep last night. That man hasn't shown up, but I've been thinking about him and Daddy all day. Sam and I are about to close and suddenly there he is. He's standing off on the path toward the Natural History Museum. It's obvious he's watching me. All of a sudden I'm a little scared, but my curiosity gets the best of me. I think I must be crazy when I tell Sam that I can finish up alone—I know she has a date tonight so I know she'll be quick to take up the offer.

"Are you sure?" she asks.

"Yeah. It's no problem. I don't want you to be late."

"Thanks," she says cheerfully as she grabs her purse and heads off toward the parking lot.

The man looks nervous too, and makes like he's going to leave, but I call out to him.

"Hey, wait."

He stops. He looks like he can't tell whether to run or not. But I make my way over to him slowly and smile.

He looks at me and says, "You've been following me."

I'm embarrassed and more than a little nervous, but I'm on a mission.

"I'm just curious," I say with a little tremble in my voice. "You know, about why you come down here."

"I'm not a pedophile," he says looking down at his feet.

"I wouldn't have come over here if I thought you were."

At last he looks me in the eye. I look at him. He's definitely not a perv. What I see there is pain. I sense that he desperately needs to share with someone.

"Do you want to talk?" I ask.

He looks hopeful and nods.

"Just let me finish closing up here."

"You need a hand?"

"That'd be nice. Thanks."

We slide the wooden doors shut and close up the booth. It's nice to have a man help with this. The doors are kind of heavy. He doesn't speak while we work. I like that about him.

"Where do you want to talk?" I ask.

"How about there?" he says as he points toward a bench

nearby. "We'll be out in the open."

We make our way over to the bench and sit a while in silence. He gets this kind of faraway look in his eyes and says, "The reason I keep coming here is that I used to take my daughter here when she was little."

"How old is your daughter?"

"She would have been twenty-nine this year."

"Would have been?"

"She died of leukemia when she was ten years old."

"I'm sorry. So you've been coming down here for all these years?"

"No. I've missed her all this time, of course, but I've only been coming down here for the past three months."

"Why now?"

"I've been having vivid dreams about her. Especially about the times we used to come here."

"And the giraffe?"

"You saw that, huh?"

"Yeah," I say embarrassed.

"I gave her one for Christmas a long time ago. It was her favorite animal. She used to love the giraffe on the merry-go-round too. It was the only animal she would ride."

"I like giraffes too. You know my dad gave me a stuffed giraffe just like that when I was that age."

"Really?"

"Yeah."

"How old is he?"

"He would've been in his fifties now."

He looks at me.

"Car accident," I say. "Drunk driver."

We're silent for a bit. Then I say, "I had a dream too. About my dad, I mean."

"Maybe we were meant to meet then," he says.

"You know, I could open the place early for you tomorrow, if you want."

"You'd do that?"

"Sure. It's the least I could do. Why don't you come down at eight."

"I will. Thank you."

***

I'm home eating dinner with Jim. I don't tell him about talking to the man earlier. I know he'd freak out if he knew I was going to meet him early tomorrow. But for the first time I notice that Jim kind of reminds me of Daddy. He's got that same thoughtful kindness in his eyes.

"You know, I had a dream about my dad last night."

He looks surprised. I don't often talk about Daddy.

"What kind of dream?"

"Well, you know how dreams are," I say trailing off. I don't really want to tell him everything—especially the bit about Daddy turning into that man.

"He died this time of year, didn't he?"

I nod, but don't say anything. Jim knows me better than to try and coax anything more from me.

"You have the whole week after Christmas off, don't you?" I ask as casually as I can.

"Yes."

"Maybe we could go to the zoo."

He looks baffled, but says sure.

***

It's Sunday and the man is already waiting for me when I get to the merry-go-round. It's foggy this morning. That's odd for this time of year.

"Good morning," he says, greeting me with a big, excited smile.

"Hi."

"What do you need me to do?" he asks.

"We have to slide the doors open," I say.

We open up the merry-go-round panel by panel.

"You know, I don't even know your name," he says as we work.

"Alex."

"I'm Carlos."

We continue to work in silence.

The doors are open now. The animals are smiling as always, but today they appear to have an extra-special effervescent sheen that defies the fog. "We're ready," they seem to say.

"I'm going to start it up. Okay?" I say.

He nods and walks up to the merry-go-round. He climbs up and takes a seat on a horse right next to the giraffe. I start it up and it starts to go around.

He's gone around once now, and I'm disappointed. I don't know what I'm expecting, but nothing seems to be happening. He's coming around again. But now for some reason the fog thickens in the air around us. It swirls like the way cream expands in hot coffee. But this fog is not like anything I've ever seen before. It's obscuring everything but the space around the merry-go-round, insulating us from the rest of the park, and it lights up the merry-go-round like a set of warm stage lights.

Carlos is coming around again, and the giraffe next to him starts to glow. It's subtle at first, but slowly the light grows and morphs. It looks like it's taking the shape of a child, and it's getting more and more substantial. Now it's clear that a little girl is sitting on the giraffe. She looks to be about ten years old and is wearing little jeans, sneakers, and a light blue shirt. She has a white cap on. I can see that she has no hair underneath it.

She's laughing loudly and waving at Carlos, calling out, "Daddy! Daddy!" He's waving at her too and calls out, "Isabella!"

Carlos gets off his horse and goes straight to Isabella. He hugs her and kisses her tiny face. She giggles and hugs him back. He stands next to her for the next couple of circuits. I hear him tell her repeatedly that he loves her as they go around again and again.

The ride is slowing now. Isabella is starting to look translucent.

I panic and wonder how I can keep the ride going, but she starts to become increasingly transparent. The ride is slowing more and all that is left now is a soft glow. Carlos steps back. The ride stops. The light fades out. Isabella is gone.

Carlos turns toward me. I see that he's crying freely. I have to fight to keep my own tears in check.

He steps down from the ride and walks over toward me.

"I don't know how to thank you," he says.

"There's no need."

"Merry Christmas," he says.

"Merry Christmas to you, too."

***

It's been several days now since Isabella appeared to Carlos, and it's Christmas morning. Jim has made pancakes. He knows how to make them just like I like them—a little gooey in the middle. We eat in silence, but I keep looking over at him. I enjoy watching him eat. We finish and leave the dishes in the sink for later.

We sit down near our little tree and exchange presents. I'm first. It's a small box. I open it. It's a heart-shaped necklace with little diamonds and rubies. I give him a genuine, open smile, and I know he knows that smile even though I don't use it often. I have him help me put it on right away.

It's his turn now. I wait to see how he reacts. It's two crystal wine goblets. He looks up at me. His eyes are watering. I can tell he's noticed that each is engraved with a single word:

"Yes."

The Box

M. L. Anderson

A small brass box sits heavy in my hands, making me remember...

Tall stacks of folded blue smocks and matching shoe bonnets.

Streaming hot water, antiseptic odors, and stainless steel sinks.

Cold fluorescent lights and blackened windows at midnight vigils.

Long webs of tubing carrying air and fluids, backed by the sound of

Screeching alarms, and the incessant beeping of monitors.

Jagged white lines dancing across grey-lit screens,

My hand on the silk of a palm-sized back,

Paper-thin skin, wrong-colored and slack,

Crimson pinpricks on pale doll feet,

Tiny fingers with no grasp to hold mine,

The blank sliver of smoke-blue eyes.

Then stacks of white papers covered in dense black type, and

Petal-colored sympathy cards strewn over table tops, and

The sweet-sour smell of wilted flowers and green water, and

The faces that came to console and the ones that didn't.

At the end, a knock at the door that had to be opened

To sign a receipt for what was placed in my hands—

The unwanted weight of a small brass box.

Still Life With a Baby

Leonora Simovonis-Brown

Tío Jose lived
inside Abuela's
pink and white armoire.
I never saw him
but Mamá did.

She was afraid of him,
his poor soul floating
in a jar of alcohol
by the will of others,
serving a lifeless sentence.

Tío José's milky eyes were closed.
His bony knees bent as if in prayer.
Ten perfect fingers curled into fists.
Pasty doll the size of a mother's breath,
suspended above a faded postcard
of Mary and her child.

"In 1492, Columbus sailed the ocean blue..."

Deborah Ramos

What if Columbus just stopped by the Cove of Caobana
for barbadine tea and a lungful of fresh tobacco,
lingering only to enjoy the uncontaminated view
and the All-You-Can-Eat-Roasted-Boar Buffet.

Any decent servant of servants
would politely excuse himself,
return home with gifts of quetzal fans
and a PowerPoint slideshow of
smiling natives, bare and unashamed,
to show the fair Queen of Castile.

Suppose bearded strangers,
saddled upon steaming horses,
did not come to conquer,
to burn heroes alive,
to feed native babies to hungry war dogs,
but came to trade pelts for pearls,
to play Cuban bingo in silver temples.
And before guests paddle
across shining water in dugout canoes,
jeweled crosses would be laid at the feet of kings
for such indigenous hospitality.

Scattered kingdoms, cupped in paradise,
would be restored, surrounded by
leafy jungles, virgin sandy edges, and turquoise lagoons,
while buried veins of gold squeeze the earth's core
to keep the planet spinning smoothly on her axis.

Imagine that everyone just sent an occasional postcard
and went back home to their
stone castles, icy dwellings, and banana leaf huts,
leaving humanity compatible with land, water, air...

an undisturbed olive soaked in a tropical martini.

Hitler, FDR, and the Banana Cream Pie

Jean Seager

Cincinnati, May 1943

Anna could have avoided the shortcut. She was, however, in a hurry to get home.

She stepped out of Hansen's Bakery, already late and feeling off-kilter. She'd promised to make an early lunch for Sol so he could get to their downtown restaurant before Irma's shift began. Irma, the pleasant, chatty waitress who seemed so promising when he hired her three months ago—he'd caught her stealing. Just a few cents at a time, but still, he had to fire her. It was a disagreeable prospect, especially during wartime, when workers were hard to get, and especially for Sol who trusted everyone. Anna thought an egg salad sandwich made with his favorite Hansen's bread—now nestled in her shopping bag—would cheer him up.

The spring sun felt warm on her shoulders. She took long strides, and her simple dress hugged her hips and swirled around her legs at mid-calf. A green suede hat, which was tastefully darker than her dress, told anyone who wished to notice that she knew how to match a hat to a dress. A former hat designer, Anna prided herself on her choice of haberdashery.

She took the short cut. It led through the alley just past Second Street and seemed pleasant enough at first. On her right, lilacs peeked over a shoulder-high fence, their branches like scallops on the top edge. Nailed to the fence's smooth dark surface, a poster of an American soldier, his parachute flowing behind him, advertised war bonds and implored people to "Back the Attack!" On a second poster, Lipton's urged her to "O-ooh taste!" their noodle soup for ten cents a package. And beside it, Campbell's proclaimed that its vegetable soup was better than any other. Dueling soups on a wooden fence. Anna walked past them contemplating egg salad.

And then she saw it—the poster that knocked her sideways. Against a pale blue background, it depicted an old man, his bony shoulders wrapped in a prayer shawl, his hooked nose covered with warts and his snarling mouth filled with yellow teeth. Dollar bills floated in the air around him. In bold italics it said, "The Jewish Beast."

Anna stared at the poster, and her vision blurred. The outline of the nose became a jagged design on a blue background. The prayer shawl turned into a blob of white.

"I'm not. I'm not a Jewish beast." The words tumbled from her mouth—a visceral response and one that surprised her. After all, she'd spent a lifetime shutting it all out, ignoring the likes of Charles Lindbergh and Henry Ford as they railed against the Jews, turning away when the women in her bridge group talked about kikes (while munching on her homemade cakes and cookies) and ignoring the restaurant customers who accused Sol of "Jewing" them. She and Sol had changed their names from Lipschitz—it sounded too Jewish—to Lewis. It was easier to be Lewis—she didn't have to endure hostile stares or whispered comments behind her back. And as a Lewis, Sol was able to buy the restaurant they never would have sold to a Lipschitz.

The Jewish beast on the alley fence rebuked her. How could she have felt at home in this Protestant neighborhood for so many years? Why did she think she could blend in? She could not. Not in a million years. Anna's stomach lurched. She needed to get home.

Almost in a daze, she put one foot in front of the other, slowly at first and then faster until she was nearly running, short of breath, her black pumps pinching her feet. The bread with its suddenly sickening odor, she dropped in the alley. She did not stop until she was inside, collapsed against her front door, safe.

"Sol," she called, her voice high-pitched and foreign to her.

"What is it, Annela? You're late." He shuffled toward her in his cabled brown cardigan.

"I'm not a... Jewish beast," Anna said. She could hardly get the words out.

"What happened?"

Anna told him what she had seen—the slogan that seeped like venom into her blood, the hooked nose, and the bread on the gravel left for the birds to pick at. She had thought telling him would help.

"Is this what the world's come to?" she asked.

"I don't know, Annela." He ran his hands through his graying hair. "I need my lunch."

"Your lunch?" Anna said, disbelieving, the poster seared into her brain.

"I've got to fire Irma today. And I can't do it on an empty stomach." Sol said.

"Do you remember Miss Owen?" Anna plopped onto the couch.

"Who?"

"Miss Owen, Lila's first grade teacher. Remember how she inspected Lila's head at every opportunity? She helped Lila take off her hat, pretending to look for lice. She never did find Lila's horns."

"Anna..."

"She thought all Jews have horns. So she kept looking. How can people believe those lies? She tried to spot horns on my head, too."

"I hate firing people. It's the worst part of owning a restaurant."

"And to think such a stupid person taught our child... how did we stand for it? We may as well have remained Lipschitz. At least that would've been honest."

"I've got to fire Irma and I've got to do it before her shift starts." Sol stood over her. She should have defaced the poster.

She should have torn it down, thrown it into an incinerator and watched it burn until it was nothing but ashes. Wouldn't a normal Jew have done that? Oh, this confounding war—confusing, horrific, ever-present. Nothing made sense. Everything was falling apart.

"I hate to bother the cook at the restaurant. You know how I hate to bother him to fix my lunch," Sol said.

"Poor Irma. She's got three children to support. What's she going to do?" Anna rocked back and forth on her heels before rising from the couch. She stumbled into the entryway, unpinned her hat and thrust it on a mirrored hat stand.

"At least Hitler's not on our doorstep," Sol said. Anna turned and glared at him, unable to comprehend how his overly round face had appealed to her twenty years ago. And those ears that stuck out—she once had found them adorable. Now she wanted to slap them, one at a time until they turned pink.

"I hate Hitler. I positively, absolutely despise him," Anna said.

"Calm down, won't you Anna? It's not like you to shout. Besides, I need my lunch."

"I don't have time to make your lunch. I'm too busy shouting, trying to get you to listen to me."

Sol retreated upstairs, and Anna closed the drapes. In the semi-darkness, she seethed. Not only at Sol, but at the restaurant that required so much of his attention, at dishonest Irma and her three children, at the poster whose image would not leave her. At herself for turning away. Always turning away. She felt exhausted and empty inside.

Sol came downstairs dressed in a coat and tie. He didn't mention Hitler again. Or his lunch.

"We're still here, you and me," he said, "That's really something, no? It'll be all right. You'll see." He gave her a hug, shrugged his shoulders and walked out the door. Anna was glad to see him leave.

She sighed mightily. A few twittering birds and the growl of a car engine sliced through the silence as Anna wondered how she would spend the rest of the day. At loose ends, she walked through an arched doorway into the kitchen. Above the sink, a portrait of FDR gazed at her, and across the room, lacy white curtains hung over a wide window. On the table, a porcelain bowl held overripe bananas, their yellow skins speckled with smoke-black blotches. She knew that despite their unsightly appearance, they were usable. Before the war and the rationing of sugar, she would have made them into a banana cream pie.

She stepped toward the calendar on the wall. It told her what she already knew—today marked a year without sugar, a year since she had baked anything. She missed the pastries, but even more, she missed the act of making them—the feel of dough in her hands, the aroma of vanilla and cinnamon, the sight of cakes rising in the oven.

She tied an apron around her waist.

"I'm going to make a banana cream pie," she declared, "and it will be the most delicious, most joyful food in the universe."

Anna began with the crust, depositing a fistful of flour and a pinch of salt into a sifter, which she held above her favorite bowl, sea-green and marred by a few chips in the top edge. She pulled the sifter's lever, then released it as flour drizzled downward and formed a smooth white pillow in the bowl. She dropped a glob of shortening on top. Then, with two knives, one in each hand, she slashed the margarine into smaller and smaller pieces.

Anna had made piecrust since she was a little girl in her mother's kitchen. She had marveled at the rhythm of her mother's hands, the grace of her motions.

Add a little shortening at a time, Annela, just a *bisl* until it feels right and Yiddish songs soaring above her. Knives clicked into the mixture of shortening and flour; never a hesitation, never a pause until she reduced the glob of shortening to pea-sized pieces, each one covered in flour, each one plump and delicate. Water, you've let the ice melt so it's cold enough, haven't you? One spoonful, then another and stir. A *bisl* until it feels right. No, not too moist, until it just begins to stick together.

From a tree outside her window, a cardinal whistled, and Anna paused to watch its red head swivel from side to side. Then she gathered the dough into a ball, cocooned it in waxed paper and set it in the icebox to cool.

Now for the shopping. Anna needed sugar, milk and a lemon. She put on her most outrageous hat, the one with multi-colored feathers and garlands of flowers. She checked the family's coupon book to be sure the last sugar coupon remained, and satisfied, stuffed the book in her handbag. Then she descended the three front steps to the sidewalk.

She hurried down the hill past two-story apartment houses, their flower boxes brimming with petunias and primroses. She looked straight ahead, ignoring the tender leaves that decorated the sycamore trees and the squirrels that climbed up and down their trunks. When she arrived at Sam's Grocery, she selected a bottle of milk and a package of sugar. But she did not see any lemons.

"We're fresh out," said Sam's daughter Margaret when Anna inquired about them. Did Margaret, the Protestant shopkeeper she'd patronized for years, believe in the Jewish beast? "If it's juice you need, we've got the bottled kind," Margaret added.

Bottled juice wouldn't be the same, not nearly as tangy as juice from a fresh lemon. Bottled juice tasted stale. Anna chose a sorry-looking lime as a substitute for the lemon in her pie.

"How's Charlie?" she asked as she approached the cash register.

"We haven't heard from him in two weeks, since his letter from the Solomon Islands," Margaret said. "But Mom believes he's safe. She prays for him every morning. And I pray on Sundays."

"Prayer can't hurt," said Anna, convinced it didn't help either.

"That'll be thirty cents, plus a sugar coupon," said Margaret.

Anna put a nickel and quarter in Margaret's hand, but the sugar coupon gave her pause. Did she want to spend her last coupon on a pie? An imperfect pie in which lime juice replaced lemon juice? Did she dare deprive Sol of sugar for his morning oatmeal and afternoon tea? He wouldn't understand her need to create this pie, and she wouldn't be able to explain it to him. She didn't want even to try.

Her hands on the clasp of her pocketbook, she imagined the dough in the icebox and the bananas in the porcelain bowl. She thought of Charlie in the Solomon Islands and Miss Owen looking for horns. She pulled the coupon book from her handbag. At the perforation, she tore off a pale pink paper about the size of half a playing card and handed it to Margaret. Then, anxious to get to the task ahead, she carried her purchases up the hill to her apartment.

In the icebox, the dough awaited her rolling pin.

Just a few passes of the pin, Annela. The fewer the better. You want a flaky crust. And lean into it. Let the dough ooze out, a precious little circle for your pie. That's enough. And scoop it into the pan, gently, gently, and open it up so it's ready to be a home for the filling. Tear off the excess dough and flute the edge. How nice it feels when you press your thumb into it, pliable yet firm, and it doesn't stick to your hands.

Anna admired her handiwork from all sides. She put the crust in the oven to bake, set the timer for twelve minutes, and turned her attention to the custard.

She squeezed the lime, which rewarded her with more than enough juice. It smelled sweeter than a lemon. How would it taste? And what would her mother think of her substitution? With the milk, eggs, sugar, and margarine congregating on the counter, she bent to get the double boiler, a special two-tiered pot necessary for cooking the custard. She picked it up and right away she knew something was amiss.

A crack, like a barb of wire, zigzagged in the double boiler's glass, from the lip to the bottom.

"Oh, no. Not this. Not now," she said, and slumped into a kitchen chair. The Jewish beast re-entered her head as she sat, her hands heavy at her sides and her shoulders sagging.

"It'll be all right," Sol had said. But he was wrong. The double boiler was useless and everything was falling apart.

The timer dinged. How dare it sound so cheerful? Heat scorched her arms and chest as she removed the crust from the oven.

"It was going to be the most wonderful pie, Mr. President, after a year without sugar. And now…"

She looked at FDR. His eyes were kind, deep-set beneath dark, full eyebrows.

"How many years until this war is over? Just tell me that. And who will win?" Anna leaned against the back of her chair, still looking at Roosevelt.

The president exuded confidence, his thin lips set in a straight line and his chin raised as if he were surveying a battlefield. "Carry on with Roosevelt," they said during the election campaign. And the nation voted for him.

"Oh you must be so tired of it all. I'm tired, too. More than I can tell you, so tired. When will it be over?"

FDR didn't look tired. He looked determined and strong and able to carry on forever.

Anna stood and straightened her back.

"If I could bring the pie to you and Mrs. Roosevelt, I would," she said. "You would like it."

She tossed the double boiler into the wastebasket. Then she removed her apron and took a shopping bag from the drawer. With her flowery, feathery hat pinned to her head, she walked down the hill to buy a new double boiler. This time she used the shortcut through the alley near Second Street where earlier she had seen the poster.

The Queen City Market did not have much in the way of merchandise. In the kitchen section, a few potholders, colorful but lonely, dangled from black metal hooks. Next to the potholders, frying pans hung above a shelf of cooking utensils. Anna found a double boiler behind the utensils. It was glass, of poor quality. She frowned and searched for a clerk.

"Do you have any double boilers that are Pyrex?" she asked.

"I'm sorry, ma'am. We've only got what's out there on the shelves."

Anna did not reply.

"They might have Pyrex at Woolworth's," said the clerk. "It's a half mile down the road."

"I know where it is," said Anna as she trudged out the door. She didn't have much hope that she'd find the double boiler a half-mile away. Why would Woolworth's have it when Queen City did not? But she'd already compromised on the lemon. She owed it to her pie to use a proper double boiler.

The shelves at Woolworth's looked more depleted than those at the Queen City Market, and after searching behind flatware, potato mashers, and scrubbing brushes, Anna settled for an inferior double boiler, much like the one she'd previously declined. Her feet ached as she carried it home.

Leaning over the sink, she washed the new boiler. The glass seemed flimsy—lighter and thinner than she preferred. But she'd make do. She filled the bottom with water, and as the water heated on the cooktop, she watched the margarine melt in the top. To the margarine, she added sugar, flour, and salt; poured in milk, lime juice, and egg yolks; and whisked out the lumps. The water bubbled, and she stirred the mixture as it became hotter and hotter. Here was the magic of cooking—combining disparate foods into something new, transforming common ingredients into creamy custard, creating a banana cream pie while the world destroyed itself.

Anna circled her dark wooden spoon round and round in the hot liquid. Afternoon sunlight filled the room. A breeze fluttered through the curtain, and the custard bubbled, thickening as it gurgled a pale sunny yellow. Anna continued to stir, knowing she must keep the spoon in motion until the custard arrived at the ideal consistency.

The breeze blew stronger. It spun the sweet smell of Anna's pie-in-progress across the kitchen. Outside the window, a fawn-colored female cardinal perched in the tree, where the red male had hopped and whistled. Anna hoped the pair would build a nest in the yard. She nodded at FDR. Eyeing the piecrust, she imagined it overflowing with bananas and custard. She imagined presenting it to Sol. She'd show it to him after dinner, before she sliced it with her special silver server.

"Delicious," he'd say. He always praised her cooking, whether the food was tasty or not. It was just the way he was. She wished she could share the pie with her mother, now of blessed memory. *Aheym, oy aheym Briderlakh aheym,* she sang. A home, a home, a place of rest. The Yiddish words came easily to her lips. Why was she singing in Yiddish? She didn't like the language and never completely learned it. But with the pie and the memory of her mother, Yiddish simply felt right.

In the middle of the melody, a sound—sharp and ominous—punctured the air. She stopped singing, stopped stirring, and nearly stopped breathing. Custard dribbled on to the stove top. Could it be? And the double boiler not one hour old?

Drops of custard splattered the floor. Shards of glass fell and splintered into pieces. The messy mosaic of yellow and white crept toward Anna's shoes. She turned off the burner and put a hand to her neck, her collarbone hard against her fingers. The room darkened. The birds yelled. The bananas stank.

Dayn mut, Annela? Her mother's voice. Where is your courage? I have no courage. A *bisl mut, Annela,* just a little. I am utterly, utterly without courage, Mama. I've always been without courage and the war makes it worse. *Neyn, Annela.* You are my bravest child.

Anna reached into the pocket of her dress. She pulled out a large paper, which she had folded several times.

When everything is falling apart, that's when courage matters most, Annela.

Anna unfolded the paper. The prayer shawl, the bad teeth, the warts, the words—she ripped them into tiny pieces.

My bravest child, Annela. A banana cream pie, so joyful. Don't make it until Hitler is dead.

With both hands, Anna flung the pieces of paper into the air. White and black and blue they fluttered about her head, her shoulders, her chest and her feet. They settled in the yellow custard on the floor.

She tiptoed through the mess, walked under the arched doorway into the front room and sat on the couch, waiting for the day to end.

An Elegant Plan

Laurie Richards

These days, the City of Lights ripples with violence. Rifle fire pops at our trucks; petrol bombs blow up our tanks. Every morning, bodies of soldiers float in the Seine. I heard yesterday that one corpse was a *sonderfuhrer,* an office worker, like me. As I make my way through the First Arrondissement, odors from putrid corpses waft toward me. I cover my nose and bicycle one-handed to the Hôtel Meurice.

At the door, a sentry says, "The Yanks are so close we can smell their hot dogs."

Who can smell hot dogs over the stench of death?

In our communications room, Johann reads a message that says Metro employees have joined the gendarmes in a strike. No trains moving; no police policing. General von Choltitz issues an order: Shoot all strikers.

As if they wear arm bands labeled, "Striker. Shoot here."

Our troops won't find them because Parisiennes became bolder after the Allies broke out of Normandy. The French harbor workers in attics over their shops, in cellars under them, behind fish carts in the Marais. These enemies wear no uniforms to let us know they are dangerous. And they are all around us, well hidden, blending in with those French who still cower.

Every day, many of our soldiers desert. *Idioten.* Do they expect a welcome back home? *Hello, Arnie. Drink some schnappes.* If they make it to Germany, they're only delaying the pincers Ruskies and Yanks have in store. Exquisite torturers those Ruskies, and I'm told the Yanks are learning fast.

I won't be there. I plan to stay in France, to blend in. My plan depends on clever timing, but it is elegant.

"Do you know," I say to Johann. "'Elegant' is the same word in German, French, and English?"

"Something else they steal from us," he says, in that whining way he has.

Johann is also a *sonderfuhrer*. He can read French well enough, but his accent is thick, inelegant. He will never blend in. In cafés, the French hunch their shoulders and turn their heads when he speaks. Thanks to my mother, I speak French without an accent. I can even speak English with a French accent, and I can pretend my German is halting.

Johann looks at my empty message box and holds out a sheaf of papers. "Otto, help me with these."

I take them. They report many skirmishes in the city. Outside, Free French troops are pushing forward with the Yanks. I glance at my watch as if I could time the exact moment of their arrival. I dash off copies of the reports and give them to a watery-eyed runner with hair the color of butter. I'm surprised this boy hasn't deserted. He can't be more than sixteen. Terror seeps from his slouched shoulders, and his fingers shake when he takes messages from me. He won't last long when the French free their city.

We know about Hitler's order to von Choltitz. Our troops cannot leave before destroying the City of Lights. The Opera House, the Louvre, Notre Dame, the Eiffel Tower—all mined. Seventy bridges are set to explode. Our Fuhrer wants Paris in rubble.

Johann is naïve. "*Der Fuhrer* would not order that," he says. "It's the generals around him."

Hah. It will be the sight of a lifetime. *I lived to see Paris die,* I could tell my children if I ever have any.

Except I will not stay to watch.

I did not arrive in Paris during the first days of Occupation, but I will leave during the last. If I wait too long, the Allies will shoot me. I do not deserve to be shot. I am only a translator; a *sonderfuhrer* is not a soldier, but the Allies would not know that. They would see my uniform and shoot. At the perfect moment, though, I will translate myself into a Frenchman. Otto Schmidt will disappear and Armand Dupois will blend in.

In my pocket are enough coins for Blonde Marie in the Pigalle bordello. *Why are so many of our horizontal companions named Marie?* I have always been generous with Blonde Marie, even giving her an expensive perfume once. It is time for her to repay me with something more than a wiggle of her butt. It's not even a fantastic butt. Those are saved for the officer bordellos.

I jostle past many other *sonderfuhrers* when I enter. Through the thin walls, I hear moans and grunts as always, although Blonde Marie says, "Not much business these days."

"Are you carping for extra payment?" I say. "I could report you. You know the prices are set."

She wiggles her shoulders. She thinks it is flirtatious. On my last visit, I confided in her that I farmed turnips as a boy. She had laughed. "I have never been on a farm. I have never been outside Paris." Then she called me *navet souffle,* turnip breath. She thinks she is witty.

Machine-gun shots rattle, clacking, as if scouring the street outside the brothel. When a grenade goes off, the walls shake. An explosion sounds, farther off, but through it all Marie stares at me with a bold disdain, her eyes squinting. As the sounds of sirens and heavy boots fade, she tells me to undress.

"Not tonight," I say.

She sneers. With her lip curled she looks ancient. It takes over her face and pulls down her nose, as if her mouth could touch it. She has always hated us. I believe she knows I do not mind her hate, and she has sneered less with me than with other customers.

"Soon you won't be coming here," she says. She sits on the bed and holds out her arms for me.

"Tonight we talk," I tell her.

"I think your future is dark," she says. "Maybe soon you won't be talking at all."

"Don't be smug. You too must worry about the future, Marie."

Her head jerks up, shoulders straight and tense. She fluffs at her blonde curls. I reach and grasp a lock of hair. I am not pulling it, but she understands the point. We both know about the *tondeurs,* the French who shear the heads of the prostitutes serving us. *Tondeurs* will throng in mobs when the city is liberated.

Where have those valiant mobs been hiding? No men ever thronged to save their women from the bordellos.

What will German men do when the Allies arrive in our cities?

I cannot care. My mother and father died last year. I have no one else to worry over, and I will not *be* in Germany to hear our women scream.

I smooth my fingers over Marie's blonde hair. "Yes," I say, "you should be concerned, but we can both avoid a dark future."

She pulls away from my touch, stares at the wall.

"You can get information, Marie. You know people." Her sister is one of the fantastic butts in the officers' brothel.

"What information?"

My time with her is almost up. The madame will be wondering, *are you finished, Sonderfuhrer?*

I tell Marie my plan. As I expected, she quickly agrees. Why not? Her role is easy. My French is impeccable, but I may need a French wife for a while. A man and wife might appear less threatening than a man alone. I show her the forged identity card that says she's twenty. "I am a magician. I've made you years younger." She shrugs.

For my disguise, I have stolen clothes and a cap from one Armand Dupois, a street cleaner. I came upon him crouching near a fountain, splashing water on his face. I watched him stumbling as he worked and followed him for days. He lived in a cellar room in the Eighteenth Arrondissement. Nobody in all of Paris will care that he's disappeared. He is one of the thousands of poor. Tens of thousands, too many to care about. We conquerors are thorough— we have made the poor more than wretched. We have made them invisible.

I have been efficient, overlooked nothing. If they find Armand's corpse, they'll not trace the murder to me.

Marie confirms the news I learned at the Meurice. She whispers. "Allies are fifty kilometers from Paris. Free French are with them." If she thought it was untrue, she would not be whispering. She would want to mislead all the *sonderfuhrers* in the bordello's rooms with tissue-thin walls. The scent of my gift perfume wafts around her as she leans toward me. She tugs on the sleeve of my uniform and drops her voice even lower. "We should go tomorrow."

I give her the name of a café. "Meet me in the morning, no later than ten," I say. "Peasant dress. No makeup."

***

The next morning, Johann arrives late in our communications room. He is pale and huffing. His uniform trousers are smudged on the knees, and a sleeve is torn at the shoulder. The runner, who has just taken a message from me, lets his mouth drop open as he stares at the dark spot blooming on Johann's crotch.

I wave the boy to leave, and after he does, I ask, "Were you attacked?"

"Chased," he says with a gasp and a hand on his chest. "They wore armbands of the FFI. I hate those Free French. I wrenched away and ran. I want the gun so I won't run next time."

A few days before, he had picked up a Ruby pistol we spotted under shrubs in a park. He held it in both hands as if it were a warm brioche. I took it from him and slipped it inside my jacket. "You don't know what to do with this," I said, and he had not argued. *Sonderfuhrers* can carry pistols, but Johann never did. Like as not, if he had tried to use the Ruby when he'd been chased, he would be dead.

I promise to bring it the next day, as if I will report for duty as normal. I have never lied to Johann before, but his body cannot keep a secret. His every word would be a fearful whine; his every movement would cry, "Otto is deserting."

By nine, the city is silent, but it quivers with the struggle for breath, poises for the release of vengeance. "The Resistance is setting up barricades," the runner says, "and more workers have joined the strikers."

"I am going to reconnoiter," I tell Johann, and I walk out of the room. I abandon my bike at the Hôtel so that Johann will think I am returning. In an alley on my way to the café, I change into the clothes of Armand Dupois. His baggy trousers and baggier shirt have the stink and color of the dung he had removed from the streets. But they are a Frenchman's clothes with a Frenchman's odor. The bagginess hides my knife and the Ruby, now loaded. After I put on the clothes, I smell like the streets. Armand's cap is encrusted with filth and reeking, but it will hide my hair, which, though I haven't washed it for a week, is still too clean for my new role. I had not realized how disgusting it would be to wear a street cleaner's clothes, but I will find safety in his stench.

I tie my uniform around rocks and drop the parcel into the Canal Saint-Martin. The streets are quiet, deserted. I shuffle as I walk, the way I had seen Armand walk to the fountain that night. I chose him for his defeated gait. He had shuffled through four long years of Occupation only to succumb to my knife in the last days.

The café is far from the Meurice, but I reach it mid-morning. Near the door, I huddle on the curb with a slump so that I look as beaten and gray as the stones. Two trucks camouflaged with branches and filled with our troops pass. No one cares about me; no one glances my way. So I am surprised to hear my name spoken by a man's voice.

"Otto."

Armand Dupois would not answer to the name of Otto, and I don't.

"I followed you. I saw you change clothes."

I recognize the whine. Johann will be relentless in his fear.

"Go away," I say in French.

He does not leave. In German, he says, "You're deserting?"

I sigh before I stand and face him. "Go away."

He shakes his head. "Take me with you."

I glare at him. His body screams, *I am German.*

He holds out his hand and says, "If you will not take me with you, give me the gun." Terror shows in his eyes, his shaking shoulders, even his skewed nose. He's still wearing his uniform, so I do not slip my arm into his. Instead, I nod for him to follow me.

Down the street, I turn the corner into an alley. A truck hurtles past the opening. When rat-a-tats sound on rooftops, Johann looks up, and I am standing behind him. He is still looking up as I stick the knife into his neck and turn it in his throat. When I push him so that he falls on the cobblestones, away from me, he is gurgling, but it does not last long. He had demanded the Ruby, so I turn him over and set it on his stomach. Armand Dupois cannot risk being caught with a gun anyway.

I expected to see horror in his eyes, but there was relief.

At least that is what I will tell myself.

When I return to the café, Blonde Marie is standing at the door. A dark scarf covers her head, and she's wearing a black skirt, black blouse. She carries a grimy satchel made from tapestry. She does not recognize me and her lip curls when I approach. She no longer looks ancient with that sneer though. Shorn of mascara and rouge and cheap ways, this is a young girl before me, perhaps not yet twenty. I put a finger to my lips and motion for her to hand over the satchel. She squints. Then her eyes widen as recognition hits.

Her satchel holds bread and carrots, a hairbrush, brassiere and panties, and the aroma of perfume. I toss out the laced panties, hand the satchel to her, and whisper that she should follow me.

Monsieur and Madame Dupois do not wait to see whether mines destroy Notre Dame, the Eiffel Tower, the Louvre, or the Opera, but windmills are burning in the Pantin as we pass through, and Marie rubs smoke from her eyes.

Near the city outskirts, I tell her our destination. She turns up her nose at the mention of turnip farms, but she says, "I've never seen Amiens."

Somehow—beside fields smelling of fresh dirt, listening to

crows cawing to each other—her small life saddens me. She wiggles her shoulders, and when the prostitute appears in her eyes again, the crows screak and fly off. I turn my head away. I think the crows were ridiculing her, but I don't know for sure. I can't speak crow.

Toward dusk, two soldiers, one young, both gangly, stop us at a barricade. Their jeep is parked off the road. The younger holds out a shaking hand and asks for our papers. The other searches Marie's satchel. He removes the carrots and drops them back in. Like a child who thinks you can't see him if he can't see you, Marie will not look straight at the guard. In German, the other soldier asks where are we going, why are we on the road? For a few seconds, I pretend not to understand and finally I say, "Ah, *oui*. Amiens," and, *"ma mere est malade."* My mother is sick.

They shrug as if understanding, and wave us on. But I worry. Marie is not good at this deception. I let her walk ahead of me, and I watch her hips sway, her shoulders wiggle. She cannot help herself, but she must learn. Armand Dupois cannot enter Amiens with a prostitute.

At dark, we bed down near hedges, away from the road. We eat the carrots and bread from her satchel. Twice, trucks pass nearby. After the second truck, she says, "Maybe we can get a ride with someone, Otto."

"I am Armand, Marie."

"Oh, yes," she says, and, although I can't see her face, I hear impatience in her voice. It's still there when she speaks again. "How long until we reach Amiens, Otto?"

"Armand."

She giggles and says, "Well, how long, husband?" I don't know the answer, but I tell her two days.

"Your disguise is good," she says, "You look like a Frenchman. Your German sounds the way a Frenchman would speak it."

"Our disguises must be like our skin, Marie."

She laughs. "I try my best."

"Not only your best, Marie. One mistake and we will both be

shot."

"Yes, yes. I understand."

No, you don't.

For a time, she is quiet, and when she speaks again, her voice sounds wistful. "Amiens," she says. "Will I like it, Otto?"

Armand, not Otto.

"Do you like turnips?" I say, then turn on my side and pretend to snore. Soon I hear poor Marie's slowed, rhythmic breaths. But I do not sleep.

In the morning, I will walk through stubbled, sun-scorched fields and hear only insects clicking and the speech of crows. They will tell no one about the corpse I leave behind.

Driving Away

E. Jacobs Burroughs

Backtracking out of Miramar Military Cemetery
to the main road away from rows of white,

upright stone and memorial walls, evoked
too much order for a day diffused with random,

cryptic memory. I drove lost on a thoroughfare
I'd traveled twenty years. Nothing looked familiar.

Cross streets, signs, shops weren't guiding me home—
but back to where I still felt freshly mowed

grass cushion my sandals, a cool breeze
brush my cheek, the clip of brine from

the sea on my tongue. I still heard a C-130
thundering off against the bugler straining

Day is done/gone is sun.

In my rearview mirror, a gauzy threshold
summoned a young couple in their twenties.

He wore a navy blue suit; she, white lace.
They stood before an altar, erect, tight,

elbow to elbow, primed to whisper "I do,"
never imagining not waking up to each other,

instead fading into shattered prisms, casualties
of war waged in his body, wilted away into

a small mound of ashes—boxed, walled inside
a row of brass-plaqued lockers. The day done.

Retribution

Zoe Ghahremani

Halfway through takeoff, the reality of what I'm doing sinks in and a shiver runs through me. *Am I willingly returning to the trap I left behind twenty years ago?*

Flight attendant places a plastic cup on my tray-table and barely fills it with tea. "Sugar and milk, sir?" she asks.

I shake my head. I'll never get used to their version of tea and always carry a few sugar cubes in my pocket. But today I want my tea bitter, a stale tea, one that smells like prison. Today, I am returning to memories that two decades of a good life have failed to erase.

The term 'exile' never appealed to me, and throughout years of life in the US, I have tried not to be like other Iranian immigrants who stick together, speak Farsi, and demand rice with every meal. I reasoned that if I ate burgers, wore faded jeans, and affected the American accent, it would be easier to adapt to my new life. When people asked, "Are you Iranian?" I would become defensive, as if with that question they also blamed me for world crimes. But when they mistook me for Spanish or Italian, I was flattered, as if these countries had no thugs, criminals, or terrorists.

It took years to feel safe, to believe that my phone was no longer tapped, that the neighbors would not report me for alcohol consumption, and that my history of working for the oil company during the Shah's reign would not put me back in jail. Two decades of a peaceful life and yet, the fear remains. Like a child attempting to touch fire, I feel the urge to do this and keep telling myself this trip is in search of my lost identity.

But there's more.

It was about a month ago when Oscar walked into my studio with a big grin on his face. "Guess what, Moe? Found a great buyer in Tehran for your work."

Tehran? I felt a tug inside. Wasn't that cord severed a long time ago? For a flash second I saw my paintings in the window of a gallery on Manuchehri Avenue and wondered if anyone would remember my name.

Oscar, a middle-aged Iranian whose real name is Asghar, is my self-assigned agent. An interior decorator, he sells my paintings to his customers for a thirty percent profit. When he said the name of the buyer, I remembered the man. He would not know me, for he must have interrogated thousands that year. That's all the revolutionary justice system seemed to do: capture anyone with an employment record for the previous government, kill most of them, and interrogate the rest. That man must have thousands of names and faces to forget while for me there was just one to remember, a bearded face, a foul-smelling breath, and a single name. He could have let me go. Instead, he made sure that for the following months a dozen others would continue to humiliate and torture me.

I've always enjoyed painting, but my education is in technology. It was life in America that turned me into a painter. The truth is, even after a decade of making my living through art, I still consider myself an amateur. In the beginning, limited knowledge of English narrowed down my chances of employment to waiting tables at the local *chelo-kebab* place, or helping in a Westwood grocery store and putting up with the attitude of rich Iranians. Teaming up with Oscar turned my life around.

I remember the exact moment it all started. Oscar had stopped by at my place for a drink when he picked up a painting of Isfahan's tiles, my watercolor reproduction of a photograph. "Is this *really* your work?" And before I had explained, added, "I know many nostalgic Iranians who'd gobble down such art," said the man who seemed as clueless about art as I felt. "Bet we could sell this to the guy who's building a ten-thousand square foot house."

I never thought my paintings were good enough to sell. With no background in art, I copied the pictures of masters, doing my best to imitate their brush strokes. Real art had to come from within, be unique, creative. That was not what I was doing. I painted to kill time.

Soon the corner of my rented space in the attic transformed into a small studio and the images I created became more than a hobby. Rich Iranians who desired a Persian touch in their Beverly Hills and Malibu mansions hired Oscar to decorate their homes. With the strict ban the new Islamic government posed on exports, my work soon found its market. The oil painting of a dilapidated blue door was no longer a remembrance of my grandmother's home, for it now offered the security of a month's rent, and the image of an hourglass-shaped *estekan* of tea with three sugar lumps meant food in my refrigerator.

Moe, this is America. Forget your education. Here, success is measured with money. Any kind of money.

Oscar sure knew his customers. He coached me on size and color selection, and picked the frames that suited a particular home. I searched among photographs of Iran for whatever triggered a memory. Persian bookstores on Westwood were happy to share their picture books. I combined what jumped off the page with the visions in my head, poured my memories on canvas, and sold them to strangers.

Paintings went, but memories stayed and grew inside of me. Money couldn't buy back the life I had lost, but my growing income made it easier to put behind the days when I had no place to sleep. The America that had changed old Mustafa into "Moe" also taught me about materialism. I now judged everything by its monetary worth. Fame made it easy to seem happy, and soon a labor of love that had filled my homesick moments turned into a flashing neon light inside my head. "Memories for sale. Buy one, get one free!"

With thousands of struggling true artists in LA, such overnight success baffled me. Cultural organizations invited me to exhibit at their events and a few Beverly Hills homes hosted private art shows. There came a time when I couldn't paint fast enough to meet the demand, so I reproduced designs with enough changes to make them seem original. I went from a miserable single room to a modest apartment and finally to a house with a garden and a swimming pool.

A few years later, my work found its way to a gallery in Santa Monica. Moe the Iranian artist had made quite a name for himself. Women were drawn to his dark eyes and salt-and-pepper hair, while the more aesthetically minded customers admired his use of turquoise in designs borrowed from old tiles of Isfahan. I never told anyone how, with each sale, I tried to get rid of another memory. It was as though with every piece that was sent away, I shed the tears that had been held back for years. They could take them all. Who needed the small window of a prison cell with its rusted iron bars? I'd painted that ten different times from ten different angles, and only when I received money in return could I pretend it was no longer my window.

Then again, some memories were harder to sell. I painted the eyes of Maryam more times than I could keep track of. Honey-colored eyes keep asking me "Why?" a question for which I still can't find an answer. She is a mirage in the desert of my life, so real, so vivid, yet forever unreachable. I can sell those paintings a million more times, but the eyes will forever haunt me in my sleep.

***

This has been a long flight. After an eight-hour stopover in Germany, I should be exhausted, but the closer we get, the faster my heart beats. The passenger sitting next to me cranes his neck for a glimpse of the view outside and seems disappointed to find nothing but clouds. He gives me a sheepish smile and says, "Not there yet, are we?"

I glance at my watch. "No, sir. It'll be at least another half hour."

Half an hour. In America, even half a day is an instant and in Iran, time probably still means nothing. I recall the filthy cell where my only clock was the beating of my heart and my calendar the lines scratched upon the wall; four vertical hatches crossed by a diagonal stroke. I'd scratched nine groups. In my head, a child's voice multiplies, "Nine times five, forty-five."

Forty-five days of questioning, forty-five glasses of stinking tea, forty-five nights of sleeping on the cement floor without permission to use the restroom... and how many lashes? Those I did not count as I often passed out before the session had ended. And yet, they found nothing against me. Nothing.

A nasal voice asks us to bring the seats back to upright position and fasten our seatbelts. Something tumbles and falls inside of me. Are we really there, or is this another one of my crazy dreams?

The voice of a clergy my mother used to hire for prayer recitals echoes in my head. I remember the crescendo of his monologue, the depiction of cruelty to Islam's martyrs, and his conclusion. "Revenge, people. Revenge is manifestation of divine justice!"

What kind of divine power would justify revenge?

I no longer know God, any god, not the cruel kind, nor the compassionate, and certainly not one who sees fairness in retaliation. Still, revenge seems to be the only means to reach a semblance of peace.

I'll sell my make-believe art to the man, and will make him pay the highest price. But above all, I need for him to show me the respect I deserved back then. Let him usher me through a reception, feed me well, and show me off to his customers. Time did nothing to heal the wounds he caused. So let his dollars buy back my pride. Let him pay dearly for his crimes.

Patches of the ground come to view through broken clouds. My fellow passenger is leaning so hard that he has almost fallen onto my lap. I let him have his moment with the view below. As soon as Mount Damavand is visible he exclaims, "Oh, how I adore your snow-capped peak!" His voice breaks, and he reluctantly leans back.

I too have longed for a glimpse of that white–capped mountain, but my heart stays with a mud alley where a stream runs through it, a garden that has two sour cherry trees. I see a blue door that leads to an old courtyard, and I see my grandmother placing her samovar on a wooden platform to serve us tea in the evening.

Few people I know will still be in Tehran, none who really matter. What am I doing here? I have no idea what to expect. The land down there is no longer mine. Then again, America isn't home, either. I smile bitterly at the thought that maybe I belong right here, mid-air, on no land at all.

Have the laws I used to know changed? I've done nothing to be afraid, but I hadn't done anything wrong back then, either. Two passports in my pocket, yet neither can guarantee my return. What happens to Moe if they keep Mustafa hostage? What if I am to rot at the skirts of beautiful Mount Damavand? Is this journey worth the risk? I don't know. But I do know it had to be done. For years I've been carrying a heavy load, too heavy, and if I don't get rid of the weight now, it will surely break my back.

En Passant

Carol Moscrip

Old men drinking from bags
sitting or standing around a large checkered board
painted on the park's smooth square
wine-wise as they evaluate the afternoon's moves
the wooden pieces as high as their knees
a rumor of voices at the capture of a knight
motionless, mute prisoners line the theater of war
only two generals but the witnesses are many
to the slaughter of undeserving pawns
with each death a mutual cry of consternation
as a bag passes by, a perpetual toast
to the last action taken in the invisible battle
against ennui mimed before their very eyes
as pigeons strut and stroll around the tiny plaza
with the same orange-eyed verve as in Times Square
perhaps there is no other wisdom than their continual
clucking at each other, no matter where they are,
bobbing of heads perpetually
like old men crowding a bar door with news
of the latest battle and death of a king

Something to Be Proud Of

Siobhan Welsh

This beaten, brown leather suitcase holds historic remnants, like a portable archaeological dig, bearing fragile and priceless artifacts. They are sparse, as most recoveries from sites are: weathered, fragmented and incomplete. They require the finder to piece them together, make assumptions and fill in the blanks, prompting more questions than answers. Much of what might be here has been scattered over time, having been thrown aside and neglected by the generation that produced it, only to be found and cherished by the generation of inheritance—me—receiving a legacy of memories that I did not create or witness firsthand.

The most obvious of the artifacts is a large, black-and-white framed photograph bearing the image of a group of somber men and boys. In the photo, they don helmets and government-issued, leather shoulder pouches containing flashlights and whistles, gas masks and hand shovels, canteens and basic first-aid supplies. They are young and old, stout and frail, a motley collection of fathers and sons, brothers and cousins, neighbors and co-workers, all clench-jawed and smile-less with grim pride and yet unproven determination. They comprise a newly formed division of civilian air-raid wardens in Belfast, Northern Ireland, at the start of World War II—all still ignorant of the gruesome tasks they will face during the Blitz.

Two faces in particular draw my attention—that of my grandfather, a slight, forlorn man of middle age—and that of my father—wide-eyed and rigid, his widow's peak front and center, as

if commanding his wavy black hair, itself, to stand at attention—
bearing the youthful, sincere, idealistic gaze of an eighteen-year-
old, ready to stand bravely in the face of an enemy.

I know the stories that accompany this picture. The accounts of
blackouts and sirens, of German planes bombing night after night,
of herding frightened people into underground air-raid shelters,
keeping them calm until the all-clear signal was given. Of digging
through the rubble above when each night's bombing was over—
first, to find the living and transport them to nearby hospitals,
then to identify the dead—either their corpses or their mangled,
dissected parts. I know of the time my teenaged father found his
dead neighbor trapped from the chin down under the debris of a
collapsed building. Of how he dug down with his hands to grab
the man's jacket only to have his neighbor's head roll away and
find himself elbow deep inside the warm sticky cavity of the man's
exposed neck and chest. Of how my father trembled and vomited
and cried.

I know of the evening that the family had been at a dance when
sirens interrupted their revelry. It was April 18, 1943. My father
waited, distraught, anxious for the bombing to end, because his
younger brother, John, had not made it to the shelter. I have heard
the story of how my father had seen them running—sixteen-year-
old John and his fourteen-year-old sweetheart, Kathleen—fleeing,
hand-in-hand, when the crowd rushed from the dance hall. Of how
my father fretted when the shelter entrance was closed and the
roll call was taken and Kathleen and John were not accounted for.
Of how he hoped they had gone with Pop to his assigned location.
But they had not. When my father found them after the all-clear
was given, Kathleen was already dead. John, still alive, was buried
beneath a mountain of brick and mortar, his weakened voice barely
audible through the ruins, calling to his older brother, "Kevin? I'm
here."

I know how my father tore nails and scraped knuckles, tossing
bricks and stones, cement slabs and fragments, trying to free John
from the entombing weight—breaking through just in time to see

John's chest expand and contract with its last breath. Of how my father lost his best friend that day, and for many years after the war, worked faithfully at his family's business—dragging his heart on a chain, in the company of ghosts—in a small hotel they called "Seaneen," Gaelic for "Little John."

There are other memories preserved in this tattered suitcase. A different photo of my fit young father dressed in his green kilt and golden sash, his black velvet apron adorned with medals, testifying to his proficiency at Irish step dancing. On a table by his side is an impressive silver cup proclaiming him "World Champion." Beneath the picture, I find the neatly folded velvet apron, musty and creased, still displaying its medals, as if to attest to the authenticity of the photograph. I unfold it and run my fingers across its surface, the velvet cool and smooth and thin. One medal is missing, some are tarnished, patches of the velvet are threadbare—as though the apron is vanishing with the memories attached to it.

I dig deeper and uncover several letters of recommendation written on various letterheads embossed with Belfast business addresses. They laud Kevin McKenna as "a man of integrity," a "hard worker" and "an enterprising young business associate." They extol his virtues to his would-be employers in America, deeming him worthy of the New World. There are certificates presented by the Irish Dancing Teachers Association of North America (IDTANA), of which my father was a founding member and former president, and from the A.D.C.R.G. (letters representing Gaelic words, which I have long forgotten) to Kevin McKenna, the Irish dance adjudicator, honoring him for his expertise and dedication to the promotion of competitive Irish dancing.

Deeper still, I find letters of thanks from a long list of New York City political candidates, all democrats, thanking Kevin McKenna for his contributions to their campaigns. I uncover a citation from the City of New York signed by Mayor Ed Koch, praising Kevin McKenna for his bravery in leading a group of office workers from the fourteenth floor of their burning building, through smoke-filled stairwells, to safety on the street below. Rubber bands encase a collection of loose desk calendar pages, each inscribed with humble, concise journal entries, revealing the grateful heart of the writer. They are produced in swirling flourished penmanship gained under the diligent, and as retold, sometimes brutal tutelage of the Irish Christian Brothers.

I must cling to these memories—the ones I have received, held in this trampled brown suitcase—or they will be overwhelmed by the ones that I experienced. The nauseating smell of days-old *Grecian Formula* and body odor, urine and tobacco, stale liquor and rotting teeth, all poorly masked under a daily baptism of Old Spice. The discovery of Scotch bottles—quarts of Johnny Walker Red—hidden under stairwells and couch cushions or stuffed inside boots in the back of a closet. The emotional weight of senseless arguments and interrogations stemming from innocent childhood comments and incidental actions. Young skin negligently burned by carelessly held cigarettes. Tender hearts heedlessly battered by spitting streams of criticism. Yelling and crying and dinner plates smashing against kitchen walls. The vision of a man whom I wanted to disown staggering and cursing and falling into the gutter, while friends and neighbors watched. Echoes of "drunken Mick" in the taunting and teasing of the neighborhood children who saw. Embarrassment. Shame. Hope succumbing to hopelessness. Hate tethered to guilt. Sadness fueling anger. Love at war with pain. Longing. For something normal and good—something to be proud of.

This Breath-filled Morning

Seretta Martin

Rivulets of dirt seep between my toes
as I water the sunflower sprouts
immersing myself in the spirit of this garden
tended for years by my father.
His warm breath brushes my shoulder
as I lean to meet the striped caterpillar
on a fig leaf. This feels like the place
Father lingers, yet he could be anywhere
without the burden of an arthritic body
holding him down. Today, all I have to do
is follow the grassy path where he walked
into the sacred-shadowed place beneath
the avocado tree we planted when I was five.
I expect that the afterlife will have plenty
of sunlight to grow trellised beans, corn
and cherry tomatoes and an allotment
of time to hear his deep voice.

The Oakland Mets

Anne Bancroft

At first I didn't want to know, of course. For two days I pretended I wasn't waiting for the appointment. I bought jeans because dying people don't need new clothes, and then spent a couple of hours on Trip Advisor, checking out places to stay in Alaska. It wouldn't get warm enough to go there, probably, for a good nine months. Nine months in the future. Planning a trip that far out would magically keep me well enough to go hiking when I got there. In the rain forest above Ketchikan, I'd hike for miles all by myself. Bears wouldn't even scare me.

The day of the appointment, I was in Starbucks at a faux Tuscan shopping mall, sipping the coffee I'd allowed to grow cold, a bitter and unsatisfying cup. The novel I'd been carrying around but not reading sat on the scratched table before me, along with my notebook for making lists. I hadn't made any lists.

Out the window and across the parking lot, a group of women were holding hands and praying. Another bitter sip.

The women were of that indeterminate suburban matron age—anywhere from thirty-five to fifty, bottoms spreading in Lands' End khakis and flowered shirts hanging loosely over waists—clothes that say they have husbands and kids and buy too much stuff at Costco. They didn't have any signs. No disgusting pictures of aborted fetuses, no "Jesus Saves" stickers, no "Pray for the checkers at Albertsons" because of low wages or anything like that. They were just praying.

Three hours was how long I had to wait. Not long enough to

make the drive home and back worth it, but long enough for the dye they'd pumped into my veins to coil its way through my body. The technician, Tarik, told me this, told me to drink plenty of water and then to come back in three hours.

"Any questions?" he asked.

Can you please tell me how fast it's growing and how long I'll feel up for a trip to Alaska? Who would you tell at this point? Why did it come back? It's been less than three years. Hell, hardly more than two. What would you say? Should I tell my daughter Marisa now, or wait, pretend it's still good until it gets bad? If I tell her, will she respond differently than when I was first diagnosed? Or will we both revert to the way we used to be? I'd hate that, so should I just pretend for awhile? What about my job? Do you believe God has anything to do with this or is it as random as it feels, just a numbers-up or numbers-down kind of thing no matter what kind of person you are?

"No," I said, "I don't have any questions."

"You know we're looking for metastases, right?"

It is the first time anyone said that word. Hearing it made me certain the cancer was in my bones.

Out the window of Starbucks I looked around at the stores in the mall, the busy ones and the boarded up ones with the "Going Out of Business SALE" signs still up. All the cars in the lot, maybe a dozen, were parked close to Albertson's. A breeze blew a white plastic bag grocery bag across the empty parking spaces, but no one was there to chase it. I thought, maybe everyone's number is up.

What a waste to be bored in a strip mall when time is all there is and you don't know how much of it is left. I needed to produce something, so I refilled my coffee, picked up the list notebook and started to write. I'm not a writer so I did what you do. I thought I was writing about the women praying at Albertson's, but that's not how it came out.

Lord, why hast thou forsaken me in the shadow of Rubio's fish tacos?

I thank you, oh Lord, for the sustenance of Texas West BBQ
pulled pork
And ask your forgiveness for stuffing the temple of my soul
till these shorts are an abomination on my thighs
I pray for the resurrection of Scrapbook World
and for the financial health of Ritz Camera, too.
Yet, surely, I shall not wander till the end of my days
in the wilderness of Tuscany Roads
Its porticos are dark, Lord, and also, fake
Lead me to the path of something better to do, Lord
Give me time, Lord, and I'll do things differently, somewhere else.
Somewhere more pleasing in your sight.

Fucking Kyle. There I was drinking cold coffee in the Starbucks contemplating the end of my life. Even if the prayer started as a fake prayer, a fun prayer, I ended up praying about the big stuff, about doing something to make up for all the years of just going along with whatever I thought people wanted me to do. All those years of barely talking to my daughter and cheating on her father and lying in a stupid PR job. All that time believing in one fantasy after the other, never even paying attention to what was real.

There I was thinking my life is over and there's only this sliver of a chance to do something good with it and the worst thing I could do with it would be to go back and obsess on Kyle. So what's the first thing I do? I email the prayer to Kyle.

I wrote him a little note saying I'm waiting for the results of a bone scan "because of some complications," and that in my boredom I wrote this fake prayer I thought he might enjoy. I pressed "send," anyway. Still hoping he'd be there and be real, that I could touch him, somehow. What an idiot. What a liar, telling myself I was so over him.

Seconds later, my email buzzed:

"*Liz, you are hilarious! Thanks for sending this. And do let me know the results of your scan. I'm sure you'll be just fine!*"

Take care,

Kyle

I dug in my purse for a rubber band. It had been months since I threw away the thick red one that helped me to quit thinking about him, the one I'd put around my wrist and snap! Forget him! Forget him and the sting of him, make my wrist sting instead. But that day in the parking lot of Tuscany Roads I couldn't even find a skinny green rubber band. I dug through my purse, the wadded up pink ribbon tissues, the Tylenol and codeine pills, shoulder-sized Salonpas, the too-many lipsticks and the purplish brown polish I kept thinking I was going to take to that new Vietnamese nail place on Twelfth.

The man simply can't handle anything uncomfortable, any hint of real pain or fear. I can't believe I used to think all that denial was just optimism, that he was just a positive guy, not a chicken-shit passive-aggressive two-faced Southern asshole.

I wanted to write him then to say for sure I was dying, even though I had no idea.

***

To think that three years ago, before I had cancer in the first place, Kyle was my big goal in life. Not my daughter, whom I barely knew how to talk to. Just Kyle, that was it. To be with him as much as I could until I could be with him for good. I honestly believed everything good would just flow from that. As if loving Kyle would keep me alive.

Damn, I needed a better goal.

I never did let myself want the perfect family, true love, meaningful work, all those fluffy wonderful jump-out-of-bed-with-a-smile-on-your-face things we all really want, things that turn out to be too big to get. Sometimes just when you think you're on a steady keel, wanting things like that can really screw you up. So instead, I made stuff up. I pretended I had those things, just with a few complications, is all.

***

The scanning office was a flat stucco building with new construction all around, looking as if it would house a frozen yogurt shop, not machines that make tumor cells light up.

As soon as I sat on the Florida rattan chair next to the fake philodendron, the intercom interrupted old Bee Gees songs by calling my name. I walked down the bright hallway and then back into the all-white room with the Metastases Hunter. He told me to get up on this very narrow table, on the skinny foam pad with a sheet stretched tight over it. He told me to lie on my back. No need to remove my clothes. And to please stay very still. I briefly wondered how they fit really fat people on that skinny table, so I asked him. I can't believe I asked him, but he was already out of the room.

I did as he said over the intercom, inhaling deeply as the table glided me inside the big plastic donut that *click-click-click-clicked* the 3D pictures of my bones. I could almost see them lighting up. A big bulbous glow right on that rib. Maybe little stars of light on my hips, my legs, my collarbone... my whole spine was lit up like an airport runway, cells all over the fucking place or maybe just that one place, surely that neon light pulsing on my rib.

I tried not to pay attention to the white plastic hovering and clicking over my face, my chest, down my legs and over my toes. I turned over on my side like Tarik asked me to, and wished I'd done a better job of adjusting my arm. I held my breath and tried to let it out slowly, slowly, slowly. Don't move, don't move, don't move no don't think about not moving.

Lying still on that skinny table as it slid into the plastic donut hole felt like giving in, making myself a specimen, allowing the machine to move me instead of moving myself. Like always, I thought. I always did what the situation called for, moving right along with the machine.

Dad got orders and the Army moved us, so I walked into the new class in the new school and did what was expected. Did it seem there was already a gregarious, brown-haired girl everyone talked to and flirted with on the way to the cafeteria? I'd be the studious one, then, and the brown-haired popular girl would accept me as her quieter, respectful friend. Next school, I'd be the outgoing one, smiling at every kid I saw, being whoever they wanted me to be. I'd marry the guy everyone else liked, and stay with him years after it was clear he didn't like me. I'd withhold myself from my daughter because I didn't know what self to offer and it scared me to get too close.

"Screw this!" I said to the plastic hanging over my face. I've lived this way for too many years and I was just starting to figure it all out. I thought cancer had helped me discover what I wanted for myself, for a change, and to quit living outside my own soul. As soon as I started figuring things out, though, I wound up lying on a table, moving with the machine.

I was about to yell, "Tarik! I'm out of here! I'm climbing off this table now! I'm getting out of this machine and running away!" But I didn't.

The clicking stopped and Tarik came back into the room. He told me to expect results on Monday, maybe Tuesday.

"Your doctor will call."

"Thank you so much," I said, as if he'd just given me a massage, as if every muscle in my body weren't so rigid I did not feel my body at all.

I was no longer thinking about Kyle.

I left through the back door, and discovered a tiny patch of unpaved nature. A rocky path lead through a bunch of dry native grasses to a small cliff, and that overlooked the barest trickle of a creek. Mossy oaks hung over the creek bank and I heard a rustling, a lizard skittering from grass to rock. The trickle of water turned from clear to muddy as it disappeared into the weedy thicket and then into a culvert, dug into the rocks below. All I heard was that trickle, and the shape of the oaks on the creek bank were so peaceful. It's weird how focused you get when you know you're going to die, focused on what's beautiful, on what's been right there in front of you the whole time. Not just focused but part of those beautiful things. You become them, if you just stay still.

I stood there for a minute or a half hour or a day, until the sun was too bright and hot and I was not the oak tree or the water, I was still in my body and had to go home.

Catherine's Blouse

Una Nichols Hynum

Vitamins roll around the place mat
coffee getting cold, I eat oatmeal.
You called it *gruel*, Catherine.
You never ate breakfast. You'd trundle
down to the bakery about noon
for chocolate donuts and a bear claw.
Bear Claw, the word nauseates me
reminds me of one my grandfather
put in the freezer, the stained nails
curled like those of a Chinese Empress.
But I wanted to talk about the blouse.

My fountain pen is out of ink, the well
out of reach. I love the *sh-sh-shuk*
when I pull the little lever.
You wrote with pen points inserted
into a cork handle. You loved the sensuous
flow of ink, the tactile joy you experienced
down to the marrow of your bones,
that bloody marrow.

In the end we couldn't keep you.

Your daughter sends me chocolate from Belgium.
I eat it reverently as if it were the host.

She sends me shamrocks from Ireland
edelweiss seeds from Switzerland.
Maybe I don't want to talk about the blouse
she sent me the one you wore before you died,
a Kleenex still in the pocket. I burned it
at the beach on my walk.
It took ten matches to start the blaze.
I couldn't wear your fragrance, you understand
or put the memory of you in the missionary box.
I hope you're not offended.

Lessons

Lizzie Wann

there is something to be said for simple
easy laughter, a song you like on the radio
a clear sky, a bright orange sunset

on these nights, when it's quiet
and sleep comes without asking
it's important to acknowledge

because elsewhere,
or maybe even here tomorrow
it won't be like this

there's something to be said for difficult
tough conversations, terrible news on the radio
stormy skies, the darkness of a starless night

on these nights, when it's too much to take
and sleep is nowhere to be found
it's important to acknowledge

because elsewhere,
or maybe even here tomorrow
it won't be like this

About the Editor

Judy Reeves is a writer, teacher, and writing practice provocateur whose books include *A Writer's Book of Days*, named "Best Nonfiction" by the San Diego Book Awards; *Writing Alone, Writing Together; A Creative Writer's Kit; The Writer's Retreat Kit* and, most recently, *Wild Women, Wild Voices*. Her fiction, nonfiction, and poetry has appeared in the *San Diego Reader; The Frozen Moment; A Year in Ink; Connotations Press; Serving House Journal; Waymark;* and *Expressive Writing, Classroom and Community,* and other journals and anthologies. Two plays, written with a women's writing ensemble, were produced by the Fritz Theater. She's also served as editor for several journals and chapbooks. She has been leading community-based writing practice groups for twenty-five years and teaches at writing conferences internationally and at San Diego Writers, Ink, a nonprofit literary center she cofounded. Her current writing project is a memoir based on an around-the-world trip she took many years ago. Judy's website is JudyReevesWriter.com where she posts blogs on The Lively Muse.

Contributors

Ann Bancroft began writing fiction after a career in newspaper journalism and political communications. She retired as communications director for the California Department of Education in 2009 and began writing personal essays, short stories, and a novel, *The Oakland Mets*. She also leads Amherst Writers and Artists workshops.

Anthony Jesse is a registered nurse, a native San Diegan, and a member of San Diego Writers, Ink. He is a conservatory-trained classical guitarist and his non-fiction works have appeared in music-related publications. "The Merry-Go-Round" is his first published short story.

Brenda Sako is from San Diego. She is a lover and advocate of character-driven stories. She loves to create complex characters that drive the plot forward. She writes short stories and screenplays while teaching English in the Los Angeles area.

Poet, gamer, technical writer, sometimes photographer, very occasional music producer, stoner, priest of nothing, twenty-first century dandy—**Brian Thedell** has found a lot of words to describe himself; he almost feels like he's got a working definition. DropBrian.com

Carol Moscrip is active in the local writing community through San Diego Writers, Ink, frequently presenting poetry and Dime Stories at open mics. She has written five chapbooks, a book of poems, *Straw,* and has most recently appeared in *bosque the magazine* (2016), *San Diego Poetry Annual* (2015), and *Mo' Joe: The Anthology* (2014).

A native of Colorado, **Carrie Danielson**'s first career was acting. She studied at the University of Colorado in Boulder and then at Neighborhood Playhouse in New York. Four children later, she became an English teacher and taught in the public schools in Chula Vista, California. Now retired, she has time to devote to her life-long desire to write.

Catherine Darby's work has been published in *The Muse Strikes Back: A Poetic Response by Women to Men, The Temple, The Long Island Quarterly, The Sniper, The Salmon,* and *5x7: A New York Anthology.* A Bread Loaf Writer's Conference participant and an Italian-American Foundation grant recipient, she was an editor for *Vox Populi Anthology/Seattle Poetry Festival;* she is currently the poetry editor of *The Coachella Review.* She lives in San Diego with her artist/physics family, and expects an MFA from University of California Riverside, Palm Desert in June 2017.

Cherie Kephart is a writer, editor, poet, and artist. Cherie's memoir, *A Few Minor Adjustments: A Memoir of Healing,* is the inspiring and often humorous story of her courageous struggle from years with an undiagnosed illness and how, at the precipice of death, she discovers much more than a diagnosis. Stay connected at CherieKephart.com

Colleen Brennan is a freelance writer, editor, and writing coach who has also worked as an indexer, translator, teacher, and linguist. A native Minnesotan, she has lived and worked in San Diego, Seattle, Boulder, Paris, Bordeaux, and Boise.

Dare DeLano writes both literary and children's fiction. Her book, *Odus and the Long Way Home,* won the 2015 San Diego Book Award (children's book category), and the 2014 Gold Moonbeam Children's Book Award. Her literary fiction was named a semi-finalist in the 2012 and 2016 Faulkner-Wisdom Creative Writing Competition.

Deborah Ramos has been evolving as an artist and writer since grade school. She is a graduate of SDSU where she studied art and costume design. Deborah is the author of the chapbook, *Road Warriors*. Her poetry has appeared in publications such as *Rattlesnake Press*, *Word Dance Literary Sexts*, *Strawberry Moon Press*, and recently in the collection, *River of Earth and Sky*. Deborah's poems are visceral, using language that is full of vision and attitude. When she isn't writing or painting, Deborah is a special education para-professional with high school students.

Diana Griggs, a transplant from England, is writing, dancing, and singing into retirement. She has been published in *San Diego Poetry Annual*, *Magee Park Anthology*, and *Oasis Journal*.

Diane Malloy, MSW is delighted to be included in *A Year in Ink, Vol. 10*. She enjoys long walks on the beach, dancing as much as possible, writing, teaching, coordinating projects, creating programs, spending time with dear ones, and loving life. Oh wait, this isn't Match.com?

E. Jacobs Burroughs practices being retired by writing poetry. Her poems have appeared in *The Forum - Journal of the Academic Senate for California Community Colleges*, *San Diego Poetry Annual*, and *A Year in Ink*.

Ellen Yaffa joined San Diego Writers, Ink in 2008, keeping a New Year's Resolution to explore creative writing as a welcome addition to professional writing during a long career in social services and community activism. A regular Thursday Writer and former board member, she writes primarily in the flash genre, captivated by the challenge to tell a compelling story that evokes emotion and grabs the reader in only 500-1000 words. Her flash pieces have been published in Dime Stories and Thursday Writers anthologies and *The Sun Magazine.*

Greg Johnson, a retired firefighter and a longtime resident of Leucadia, had a short story published in *Flash Quake.* The online literary quarterly went belly-up immediately thereafter. He's happy to make his print debut in this publication and prays that this story won't have the same effect.

Raised on a tiny, New England peninsula, **J. Dylan Yates** received her BFA from the University of Colorado at Boulder. *The Belief in Angels,* Yates's debut novel, was written over the course of many years while she worked a number of BFA-related jobs, including: waitressing, teaching, corporate training, real estate, nursing, interior design, directing, acting, producing, library science, parenting, and reluctant housewifery.

Jan Thompson has been writing seriously since 1993. She has published five stories in writing journals during the past several years and earned her MFA in genre fiction from Western State Colorado University in 2016. She is now working on a post-apocalyptic novel that she hopes to finish by the summer of 2017.

Jay M. Mower is a retired advertising professor and marketing executive. His poems have appeared in *Acorn Review, Chaparral, Muddy River Poetry Review, Magee Park Poets, San Diego Poetry Annual,* and been recognized in *Atlanta Review* International Competition. His chapbooks are *Light Medium Dark, Different Voices,* and *Along the Way.* JayMMowerPoet.com

Jean Seager is a California native who has lived in the same house for thirty-nine years. She is writing a book of short stories about American Jewish immigrants in the early twentieth century. A mother of two and grandmother of six, she enjoys hiking and playing competitive bridge.

Jill G. Hall, author of *The Black Velvet Coat,* is now obsessed with finishing her next novel. Her poems have appeared in a variety of publications including prior *A Year In Ink* anthologies. She enjoys helping to curate the art shows at Inspirations and The Ink Spot Galleries. JillGHall.com

Jill Murray, her husband, and cats recently moved from Virginia to La Jolla. She has a Master of Arts degree in International Commerce. She writes young adult novels with strong female representation. When not writing, she is a social activist and a volunteer with UCSD's English-in-Action program.

Krishna Jagannathan was born in India but has lived virtually all her life in the United States. She majored in English literature as an undergraduate and loves reading. Her favorite genre is historical fiction, particularly British literature. She is a private tutor, helping students in many subjects, including English and history.

Laurie Richards writes, teaches, and practices law in North County. She enjoys delving into Southern California's vibrant writing community through workshops for the Osher Institute and the Pasadena City Library One City/One Story event. Her short stories and novels cavort between horror, mystery, children's, and mainstream genres.

Leonora Simonovis-Brown is a bilingual writer who grew up in Caracas, Venezuela. She currently lives in San Diego where she teaches Spanish and Latin American literature at the University of San Diego. She has published academic articles and literary essays in several national and international journals. She also has two new poems forthcoming in *The American Journal of Poetry* and the 2016 *San Diego Poetry Annual.*

Lizzie Wann's work appears on CDs (*A Wing & A Prayer* and *A New Leaf*), in chapbooks (*Familiars, Naked Wrists, Complicated*

Skies), and in anthologies including *Comstock Review, So Luminous the Wildflowers,* and *Don't Blame the Ugly Mug.* She founded the Meeting Grace house concert series which ran from 2000-2008.

M. L. Anderson lives on a hill overlooking the Cleveland National Forest with her family, pets, and visiting wildlife. There she spends her time reflecting on past experience, enjoying the present, and conjuring up speculative fiction about the future and worlds far, far away. Her musings can be found at MLAndersonAuthor.com.

Marty Eberhardt spent her professional life as a botanical garden administrator. In retirement, she enjoys using the right side of her brain. She has published seven poems and is seeking representation for her first novel, *Holding the Line,* excerpted here. She is now working on a botanical garden murder mystery.

Michael W. Berns, PhD, is the Arnold and Mabel Beckman Professor at UC Irvine where he is the Founding Director of the Beckman Laser Institute. He is Adjunct Professor of Bioengineering and member of the Institute for Engineering in Medicine at UC San Diego. He has pioneered the use of laser scissors and tweezers to manipulate cells and their organelles.

Penny Wilkes, MFA, is an educator, writer, and photographer. She has published in a variety of genres from travel writing to animal behavior. Poetry collections include *Whispers from the Land: Travels in Spain, In Spite of War,* and *Flying Lessons.*

Regina Morin is the wife of a retired aerospace engineer: he agrees not to write poetry as long as she agrees not to repair the garbage disposal. They have lived in the Ocean Beach zip code for fifty-six years. Her poems have appeared in *Visions Magazine, America Magazine, San Diego Writer's Monthly, McGee Park Poets Anthology, A Year in Ink,* the *San Diego Poetry Annual,* and the *Reader.*

Ruth Roberts wrote plays on love and adventure as a child and performed them on her front porch with her sisters and friends. She published a limerick and short story in high school. Since then she has taught writing and literature in junior high, high school, community college, and university programs for twelve years. Currently she writes and publishes journal articles and books on diabetes and technology, specializing in insulin pumps and continuous glucose monitors. She also runs a popular diabetes website and web store. "Killin' Chickens" is the first chapter from her third novel, *Anarchy*, a fictionalized story of her ancestors in Kentucky around the Civil War. She just completed a certificate in novel writing from San Diego Writers, Ink. She lives in San Diego with her husband, John Walsh.

Sandra Yeaman has lived and worked in twelve countries. "The Students Who Never Came to Class" is a vignette from her year of teaching English in Iasi, Romania. She is working on a memoir of life in Iran, her first experience working outside the United States. Sandra blogs at SandraYeaman.com.

Sandy Robertson lived a peripatetic life in China, Japan, New England, the Midwest, Washington DC, the Bay Area, and Spain until she came to San Diego to pursue graduate study. She has made her home here ever since, happily.

Seretta Martin, author of *Foreign Dust Familiar Rain* and *Overtaking Glass* (forthcoming), is the managing editor of the *San Diego Poetry Annual* and founding co-editor of *Synesthesia Literary Journal*. She is a Philip Levine Prize and Washington Prize semifinalist. Her publishing credits include *Serving House Journal, Web Del Sol, Poetry International, Margie, Modern Haiku, A Year in Ink,* and *San Diego Poetry Annual*. She teaches poetry at San Diego Writers, Ink, California Poets in the Schools, and the Border Voices Poetry Project and has hosted the New Alchemy Poetry Series for sixteen years. Seretta holds an MFA from SDSU.

Siobhan Welsh holds a master's degree in counseling psychology and shares life with her husband in Southern California, where she serves as a mental health professional in San Diego and Riverside counties. She employs journaling, personal narrative essays, memoir, and poetry as vehicles through which she and her clients may process and make sense of their lives and experiences.

Tania Pryputniewicz is the author of *November Butterfly* (Saddle Road Press, 2014). When not making poetry, movies, or blogging at Tarot for Two and Mother Writer Mentor, Tania teaches a monthly poetry workshop for San Diego Writers, Ink. Poems are forthcoming in *Everyday Haiku* and *The Journal of Applied Poetics*.

Tim Calaway resides in San Diego. He brings his varied experiences to life in his poems and stories of lost loves, lost dreams, and lost fortunes. His work has been seen in several anthologies, including *A Year In Ink, Volume 8*.

Una Nichols Hynum was born in Providence, RI. She is a graduate of SDSU and was nominated for the Pushcart twice. Her most recent book, *At the Foot of the Staircase,* is self-published. Member of Oasis and Bluestocking Poets and Southern California Haiku Society.

William Harry Harding has written three novels—*Rainbow, Young Hart, Mill Song*—and a children's book—*Alvin's Famous No-Horse*—all from Henry Holt. He publishes the *San Diego Poetry Annual* and chairs the San Diego Entertainment + Arts Guild. His recent short stories and poetry have appeared in *The Paterson Literary Review*.

Zoe Ghahremani is a writer and artist. Her first novel, *Sky of Red Poppies,* was a 2012 One Book, One San Diego selection and is now translated to French and Persian. *The Moon Daughter* was a 2014 San Diego Book Awards winner. She is currently working on her next novel, *The Basement*.

About San Diego Writers, Ink

San Diego Writers, Ink, serves as a hub for the literary communty, promotes literature, provides artistic development for writers at all levels, and facilitates artistic collaboration. A 501(c)(3) nonprofit organization, SDWI offers classes, groups, workshops, readings, and other literary events at The Ink Spot and other locations throughout San Diego County.

> San Diego Writers, Ink
> www.SanDiegoWriters.org
> The Ink Spot
> 2730 Historic Decatur Road, Suites 202 and 204
> San Diego, CA 92106
> (619) 696-0363

A Year in Ink, an anthology published each year by San Diego Writers, Ink, represents a sampling of our community's most brilliant work. Each volume includes shorts stories, novel and memoir excerpts, creative nonfiction, satire, flash fiction, poetry, and more. The authors are a diverse group of young and old, new writers and much-published veterans. Several have had work in previous anthologies, most have been published in other literary journals, and a few allow *A Year in Ink* the honor of showcasing their first publication.

Explore the complete *A Year in Ink* collection available at our website.

A Year in Ink, Volume 1 (2008), edited by Thomas Larson

A Year in Ink, Volume 2 (2009), edited by Sandra Alcosser
and Arthur Salm

A Year in Ink, Volume 3 (2010), edited by Roger Aplon
and Jennifer Silva Redmond

A Year in Ink, Volume 4 (2011), edited by Jericho
Brown and Laurel Corona

A Year in Ink, Volume 5 (2012), edited by Brandon Cesmat
and T. Greenwood

A Year in Ink, Volume 6 (2013), edited by Michael Klam
and Anthony Bonds

A Year in Ink, Volume 7 (2014), edited by Shadab Zeest
Hashmi and Jim Ruland

A Year in Ink, Volume 8 (2015), edited by reg e gains and
Dean Nelson

A Year in Ink, Volume 9 (2016), edited by Bonnie ZoBell
and Sydney Brown

A Year in Ink, Volume 10 (2017), edited by Judy Reeves

www.ingramcontent.com/pod-product-compliance
Lightning Source LLC
Chambersburg PA
CBHW070929250626
47159CB00009B/3174